Personal Help for Girls

Nurturing a Sweet and Virtuous Spirit

From PEARABLES

Written by
A. B. Leaver

Printed in the United States of America.

PEARABLES
P.O. Box 1071
Mukilteo, WA 98275

For free samples visit:
www.pearables.com

Table of Contents

INTRODUCTION

PERSONAL HELP FOR GIRLS has been a project that we have delighted in producing. We believe every Christian girl should study and read this book as many times as possible, especially the Bible study that is listed at the end of each chapter. It is written with the thought that God has specifically created girls to a special calling of motherhood. That it is so important that we train them at a very young age to develop certain habits and skills needed to complete this wonderful task in order to train future generations.

PERSONAL HELP FOR GIRLS is for tomorrow's mothers. It is our deepest hope that our daughters will be given the knowledge of how important the task of motherhood is and how this job cannot be delegated to others. We pray that this will just whet their appetite towards womanly duties and that from here they will go on to study and develop themselves more. That they will have their hearts at home with their own children, husbands and family when they marry.

Our heartfelt prayers to each of the mothers and daughters who will open these pages and study the contents in hopes of developing Godly character that will effect the generations to come...

HOW TO USE

PERSONAL HELP FOR GIRLS is designed to be read in Chapter Studies. We have found that it works best if the mother and daughter, or two or more young girls, work together. Many have read just one chapter a week as a weekly Bible study and then used the Bible study listed at the end of the chapter as a discussion tool.

We suggest that each chapter be completed consecutively. Please finish the whole chapter, including the Bible study, for this is where it is bathed in the Holy Scriptures.

Mothers, again, we urge you to participate if you can. PERSONAL HELP FOR GIRLS is a wonderful tool you can use to grow together with your daughters in CHARACTER BUILDING.

We pray that you will be encouraged and enriched by this Character Study.

Yours in Christ,

PEARABLES

Chapter One

What Type of Woman Will You Become?

Dear friend, this book was written in hopes that it might help you become content with the role God has given you as a female. Right now you may not have really thought about what it means to be a girl, but by the end of the book, we pray that you will be so thankful that God has made you just as you are!

In the beginning God created male and female. If you look around you, you will see that there are many females in your life. Your grandmothers, your mother, your aunts, your cousins and sisters. Take a good look. Women have a lot of different stages that they go through as they age.

Something that you may never have considered before, is that you will one day grow up just as your mother did. You are a young girl now, but someday you, too, will grow up to be a woman.

From the study of God's creation we learn that flowers are grown up seeds; that cats are grown up kittens; and that dogs are grown up puppies. Women are grown up little girls. God has created it this way with all of His creatures.

How we are trained, matters a lot in how we will turn out when we grow up. Did you know that a tiny, starved, neglected, and abused puppy will grow up to be a sneaky, cowardly, or vicious dog? And the same thing goes for little girls. If a young girl is not trained to work, study, and do what God says to do, she will probably grow up to be a lazy, selfish, and ungodly woman.

We find that God has this natural law whether dealing with seeds, kittens, puppies or girls. If they are not trained up according to the laws and Word of God, they will not know the right things to do as adults and may make many wrong choices.

Another example God shows us is one of producing a good tree, one that is straight and shapely, which gives shade or bears large, luscious good fruit. In order for it to bear fruit, we must give it proper care and training, when young. Also, in order to develop a beautiful, kind, and caring dog, we must give it proper care and attention when young. If you wish to have a pony with elastic bearing, beautiful form, gentle in disposition, well gaited, a fast traveler, then we must feed, care and train her well when young.

God makes no exception in dealing with a girl and a woman. If a girl wants to become a wonderful, happy, woman of God, she must be willing to be carefully trained and taught. Becoming a strong, lovely woman of God doesn't just happen. It takes God living in your heart and then the desire to live a life pleasing to Christ. This will enable her to reach high ideals and to make a difference in the world for her Lord and Master. This must be encouraged daily to grow inside of her.

And most importantly, she must be willing to *submit to be trained* and taught by those who are older, wiser and have had more experience in the Word of God than herself.

Who do YOU Imitate?

All girls want to imitate women they admire. They look at someone beautiful and decide because of their beauty that they want to be like them. The sad thing is, many times women with outward beauty do not have inner beauty, which is much more lovely than outer beauty.

Let's take an example of a magazine model. On the cover of that glossy magazine, she may seem to have everything together. Maybe she is perfectly thin, delicate and lovely on the outside; but, she may have some bad habits which no one knows about on the inside. Habits which harm her and would be harmful to those who would associate with her. Her beauty is only skin deep.

It seems almost natural for a girl to admire such a woman, to mistake her beauty for true loveliness in Christ, thinking that if she could copy her in figure and form and actions, it would make her as beautiful as she appears to be. But this is deceptive!

There was a young girl, whose family allowed her to go to the movies where she saw a beautiful actress as the leading lady. This woman seemed to be all that a woman could be. She was beautiful to look at, had lovely clothes to wear; said all the right things; was witty and talkative; and she was sought after by all the leading men.

The young girl was impressed by the actress on the screen. She read about her in the movie magazines and bought all the tabloids with articles about her. The girl even copied her clothes and her hair. Later, it was found out that this movie star had five husbands and was currently living with a new boyfriend. That this beautiful actress drank alcohol constantly, and lived a wild party life.

Is this an example that a young girl should have paraded before her? No! Beauty must be taught to be more than outward appearance. Beauty is much more than how we look. True beauty is found in what we do.

Don't Imitate Someone Just Because They're Older!

There was another young girl whose cousin came to stay with her for a while. The cousin hadn't been trained as the young girl had been and was allowed to do many things that she wasn't. The younger girl had been taught that dating wasn't allowed in her family and that she was to not follow after the world and its ways regarding infatuations with boys. The cousin, however, wasn't taught this, and she was constantly talking about "this cute boy" or "that cute guy" whom she'd just seen when going shopping. The younger girl would watch and listen to this behavior and one day started looking at boys with the same intent as her cousin!

Be Careful of Who You Let Influence You!

Perhaps you will meet with few greater temptations in life than the desire to look at boys. Many beautiful girls, you know, will look at boys and they may even try to get you to do so too! Occasionally, you may see girls from church or even an adult do this!

No girl wants to imitate the weird, ugly, mean girl. Most young girls want to be like the beauty who is dresses fashionalbly and wears nice clothing. The good looks and appearance, the fashionable clothes, can deceive young girls into thinking that bad behavior is all right, simply because they are doing it. But, dearest friend, we are not to admire *these* girls, as God's Word teaches us. We are not to copy someone's hair style or clothing or something that just looks good on the outside! Rather, we are to copy what someone does. We are to copy beautiful actions!

Any type of a girl can look beautiful on the outside, have what the world calls a "good time", destroy her body, debauch her mind, become a victim of moral disease, die and never be missed, and never be used by God. It takes a girl with a strong, healthy mind, a pure heart, a clean life, and a godly determination. Most importantly, it takes a strong belief in God through Jesus Christ to become a jewel of a girl.

Yet, every girl needs more than a strong will and the help of her family, if she is to resist the temptations that are going to confront her in life. She must live in Christ. She needs help from God day and night. A faithful girl is the foundation for a faithful woman.

In the following chapters we will be talking about being feminine. And not only being what the "world" calls feminine, but rather what the "Word" tells us is true femininity.

Many times we will have thoughts about womanhood that we have gotten from philosophies that are against Christianity. Sometimes we don't even know that they are wrong until we line it up with God's precious Word! This is called "renewing our minds".

When we become believers in the Lord Jesus Christ, God starts to wash our minds with new thoughts. We do this through reading the Word of God, God's handbook for us to follow while we live here on earth.

In the following lessons, some things you might learn will be in direct contrast to what you have heard the people of the world teach. One important thing to always remember is this:

"ALWAYS LINE UP EVERY THOUGHT TO THE TEACHINGS IN GOD'S HOLY WORD, THE BIBLE."

The world may say one thing, but the Word will say another.

****

Discussion:

(Dear Parent, most of the questions are covered in the chapter, so we left the answers up to you. If the questions were not covered in this material, we gave a small tidbit of thought in order to help.)

~What is an "influence"?
~Can you think of any Scriptures that teach us regarding influences in our lives?

Read: "A companion of fools shall be destroyed." Proverbs 13:20
~Why should you not follow after false beauty?
~How does this Scripture relate to allowing females without God to influence you?

Read: "Meddle not with him that flattereth with his lips." Prov erbs 20:19
~What does flatter mean?
~Why do you think the Scriptures would tell us not to have anything to do with a person who flatters?

Read: "One sinner destroyeth much good." Ecclesiastes 9:18
~Do you have any movie stars that you admire?
~Why do people admire them? (Usually because of their out ward appearance.)
~What's the difference between outward and inward beauty?
~Who should you admire? (Godly women who try to live the Word of God.)

Chapter Two

WHAT DOES IT MEAN TO BE BEAUTIFUL?

The Truth of What True Beauty Is

As very young girls, we are taught that prettiness is so important to the world we live in. From infancy, strangers will come up to us and coo and pinch the cheeks of a beautiful baby. A darling little girl with golden curls and blue eyes of the age of three will usually get suckers or treats from the clerks at stores.

Outward beauty seems to give rewards that are dependent only upon HOW beautiful we are. This is *not* right. This type of attitude shows respect only for outward beauty. God tells us not to do this.

You might have seen in your young life, a beautiful girl on the outside, who is mean on the inside; when you play with her, she is selfish, loud, and bossy. Her only intent is to get her own way. She is no longer beautiful; but, has become totally unattractive. This is because she doesn't have the inner beauty which really counts.

The Truly Beautiful GIRL

In the beginning God created mankind, male and female. First, it is important that we learn that there *is* a difference between being male and female. Women and men were not created the same. God created them with different functions and duties. He created them with different forms on the outside, and also with different ways in which they tick on the *inside*.

While the world around us tells us that there is no difference between women and men, we as Christians know that this is not true. There is a difference! And it is something wonderful that we should embrace!

Males were created by God to be strong. He made them bigger than most girls. They are masculine. Their voices are deeper and lower; their muscles are formed stronger than females; and their attitudes and personalities are masculine. This is because the man was to be the head, or the "leader", of the female.

The Scriptures tell us, *"But I would have you know, that the head of every man is Christ; and the head of the woman is the man; and the head of Christ is God." 1 Corinthians 11:3*

On the other hand, females were created by God to be a "helper" to the man. That doesn't mean we are inferior by any means. No! Being a helper is a wonderful position to relish in.

Don't you love to help your mother when she needs it? Don't you love to be useful to others when they are in need? Females were created by God to give. We are the "givers"; the "caretakers" of the males. What a wonderful and awesome responsibility!

God created males physically to take care of and lead females. We are smaller than they are; more gentle; softer; and we need to learn to depend on those who are stronger. In return, we help them and care for them. We are so blessed by God to be given a life full of unselfish duties. This is where true happiness comes from.

We are not men. We do not have the same duties that men do. Our Heavenly Father created us to be "wo-man", the man's helpmate.

Standing for God's Truth

Are you thankful that God created you female? You should be very thankful! God has made you for a specific purpose.

It is very important that you understand that your purpose in life is not to be the most physically beautiful form for every one to look upon. That would be vanity. The scriptures tell us: *"Favor is deceitful, and beauty is vain; but a woman that feareth the Lord, she shall be praised!" Proverbs 31:30.*

We need to stand against worldliness. *James 1:27 tells us: "Pure religion and undefiled before God and the Father is this, To visit the fatherless and widows in their affliction, and to keep himself unspotted from the world."*

As a young woman, it is so important that you understand that one way of keeping yourself unspotted would be to shun worldly thoughts of womanhood.

Remember, the world, or our society, will tell you one thing, but God says another.

Let's list a few of the *false teachings* today:

~ The most important thing is "how you look" on the outside.
~ Being concerned with what others think and say about you.
~ Having a career outside of your home and providing for your family.
~ Your security is in your career.
~ When you marry, you will not submit to your husband, but be his equal.
~ Dating, or trying out, different boys is how you find a husband.
~ Having a good "self image" is all important.

These are just a few things you might encounter with people in the world. You may even find these philosophies amongst close family members. But as a believer in Christ, you must learn to replace these thoughts with what the Bible tells us. For each of these thoughts, God has a response of what He would will for you! We'll go over each of these in the discussions coming up.

You, sweet girl, will need to stand for your beliefs. This doesn't mean that you take a loud platform, as this wouldn't be very lady like, but it means that you will DO what God has called you to do. Many people can "say" that they believe things. This is where we get confused. But you can tell more about what people believe by what they "do". You must be a DOER of the Word of God. Then you will stand for His Truth!

Why True Beauty is Needed in our Day and Age

If you take a look around you, you might see many girls whose faces are painted just perfectly, they do not have a hair out of place, they are dressed in the latest fashions and very stylish. However, they might be deceived into thinking that this is true beauty.

God has called us to a different way of thinking. He has called us towards beauty of a different kind. **One that lasts.**

Take a look a your grandmother, for instance. She, too, was once a beautiful young girl on the outside. But what happens to all of us? We age! Right now your body is aging and it is soon going to look just like that of your grandmother's! But do you think your grandmother is any less beautiful? Of course not! Because of your love for her and hers for you, every familiar crease and wrinkle on her skin is lovely to you and all those who love her. Her enduring times of listening and taking care of you and your parents have caused her to be beautiful in your eyes.

True beauty is that which is inside. Right now you need to start developing the beauty which never fades. That of a faithful and loving heart, and a spirit that reflects your love of God. This is what the world needs to learn today. Not to place our hopes and security in our outward appearance which will quickly fade. You need to start being an example of Christian femininity right now, as we speak. This is a way to let your light shine for Christ.

****

Discussion:

~What things have you thought make you beautiful?
~Name one person whom you think is beautiful.
~List at least seven things about them that make you think they are beautiful.

~Which of the things you listed are temporal? (Things that are just temporary.)
~Which of these things will last throughout eternity?

Read: Matthew 23:27

The following thoughts of the world are opposite of what scriptures teach. Talk about each of them and then discuss what the scriptures tell us afterward.

~ The most important thing is "how you look" on the outside.
"Thus saith the Lord, 'What iniquity have your fathers found in me, that they are gone far from me, and have walked after vanity, and are become vain?'" Jeremiah 2:5"
~ Being concerned with what others think and say about you.
"Woe unto you, when all men shall speak well of you! for so did their fathers to the false prophets." Luke 6:26
~ Having a career outside of your home and providing for your family.
"That they may teach the young women to be... keepers at home (homemakers)." Titus 2:3-5
~ Your security is in your career.
"But we had the sentence of death in ourselves, that we should not trust in ourselves, but in God which raiseth the dead." 2 Corinthians 1:9
~ When you marry, you will not submit to your husband, but be his equal.
"Wives, submit yourselves unto your own husbands, as unto the Lord." Ephesians 5:22
~ Dating, or trying out, different boys is how you find a husband. Read Genesis Chapter 29 & 30, the account of how Jacob had to go through the father, and the father protected his daughters even through marriage.
~ Having a good "self image" is all important. A good "self-image" is nothing but having PRIDE in oneself. *"Every one that is proud in heart is an abomination to the Lord." Proverbs 16:5*

Chapter Three

THE FEMININE PERSONALITY

Have you ever seen a true lady? What are the qualities of a "lady", so to speak? Do you even know what a "lady" truly is? The dictionary tells us that it means "a woman having the refined habits, gentle manners, and sense of responsibility often associated with breeding and culture. To be "ladylike" means: "Characteristics of a lady; delicate; refined; well-bred."

This is very interesting. To have breeding or to be well-bred, means that you have been well trained. It means that you have been trained in the gentle arts of being a woman. You have been taught to be feminine. This is what we are going to learn throughout this book. The art of being feminine!

Take a moment to think on what you believe it means to be feminine... What is true femininity to you?

Femininity is a softer, gentler quality that a woman has in all of her actions. She is opposite to the male. She is feminine in her manners, in the way she moves, in her personality, and also in her outward appearance.

Your Movements

Do you think there is a specific way that men and women walk? If you put a large, gawky man in a dress and high shoes, what would happen? Well, most likely this man would still move like a man. He would probably fall off the shoes, he would move stiffly and uncomfortably.

Now, how do ladies walk? They move gracefully, smoothly, and femininely. This is what you, too, must learn. The art of moving as a lady would.

Again, remember, CONTRAST. You must remember that God would have a woman move differently from a man. Usually this is inborn, but occasionally, there will be some young ladies who have developed very manly characteristics and who might need help in describing how to have feminine movements.

A lady always touches others softly. She would never be gruff or rough with her hands. When shaking hands, she would never shake them with an expression of strength. To do so would be manly. When a young lady is making a point, she would never hit something emphatically, but would do so with gentleness only in her speech.

When moving, remember MODESTY. A lady moves gracefully, with light, fluid movements. Her steps are smooth and her body is held straight.

A feminine girl moves with graciousness in every bone of her body. She does not move roughly or stiffly like a man, but shows femininity in each of her steps.

Outward Femininity

Many people will say that it doesn't matter how you look on the outside... It's what's on the inside that counts! Is this a true statement?

If we only go by what the Word of God says, we will find that God has something to say about the outward appearance of women and men.

"The woman shall not wear that which pertaineth unto a man, neither shall a man put on a woman's garment; for all that do so are abomination unto the Lord thy God." Deuteronomy 22:5

According to this scripture, it sounds as if God might care a bit about our femininity. It seems that God would also want women to be feminine in their dress and men manly in their outward appearance also.

God doesn't also stop with just clothing, either. He talks about hair, too. For thousands of years it was *normal* for women to grow their hair long. It is strange and manly for women to chop off their locks and have their hair look the same as men. God mentions in the Bible that He would like women to have long hair and men to have short.

"Doth not even nature itself teach you, that, if a man have long hair, it

is a shame unto him? But if a woman have long hair, it is a glory to her; for her hair is given her for a covering." 1 Corinthians 11:14-15

"But if it be a shame for a woman to be shorn or shaven, let her be covered." 1 Corinthians 11:6

But, we do not want to become harsh and condemning regarding our obedience. Ask God what He would have you do with your hair. He will give you an answer, and remember, what is long to someone else, may not be long to you. Remember the most important thing, LOVE ONE ANOTHER.

Isn't it interesting that God has created us feminine even in our very appearance? He would have us wear clothing that only women wear, and he would have our hair long as a covering and a glory! Isn't this wonderful? We are to be feminine in every aspect of living. God created it this way. This is His will.

Being feminine is to place a great importance on the differences between men and women. It is to make a line between what a woman is compared to what a man is.

Just as men would never wear elaborate, frilly, lacy type clothing, true ladies would never wear clothing like men's. They would play on the contrast! They would not dream of wearing any type of clothing that resembled a man's. A true lady likes to dress in the most opposite fashion from a gentleman.

You might consider what a group of beautiful girls are doing in one church in California. They believe that ladies' clothing should be softer, lighter, and never created out of the same fabric that a man would wear. They believe that females must be modest and reflect a woman of God.

These sisters try to make dresses or purchase them if they are sewn out of materials which are not made for males such as those materials used in blue jeans, which have always been for males; those for creating work suits; those for work clothes. Some Christians believe that dark clothing has always been for men, while women whose aim is being feminine, have sometimes worn whites, pastels, or soft and tiny flowered prints. Femininity might be shown through soft materials also, rather than stiff clothing of working men.

However, this must be an individual choice as God leads you, not men.

Ask our Heavenly Father what He wants your own particular style to be as you grow in His ways. You may like to buy denim jackets and go crazy with it by decorating the edges, glueing lovely trinkets all over and making something dreary into something beautiful and feminine!

If your parents have allowed you to wear pants, you should try to soften this by adding feminine apparel, such as a crocheted, frilly collar to your blouse; a soft scarf; or a ribbon tied around your blouse collar in a pretty bow. Be creative! Use those accessories to your female advantage!

One important thing to remember about Christian femininity is that God wants us to be MODEST. God would not have us expose our bodies to anyone. We are to keep them covered and to not call attention to our physical form.

Any clothing that is too tight, or too revealing, or that calls attention to our physical form in any way, should be immediately placed in the trash bin.

This includes our underwear. We should never allow our slips to hang or to have any part of our underwear show (such as a bra strap) beneath our clothing.

Keeping an attitude of modesty helps the males around us think of us as their lovely sisters in the Lord.

How You Speak

A young lady might want to keep her voice gentle and calm. Not too soft, so that she cannot be heard and then becomes irritating, but with just the right tone. She must speak pleasantly, and with love and kindness.

A lady must remember that she must not talk with any of the qualities of a man. She would not be emphatic over what she says, but when she is talking about something important she will state what she has to say gently.

Remember not ever to talk too arrogantly. Arrogance and "self-assuredness" is not what God calls humility.

How we speak femininely is not only in the tone of our voice, but also in WHAT we say. God's feminine girl is always thoughtful of others and avoids being inconsiderate or rude. She is polite and tactful in all situations.

A sweet daughter of Christ would never use bad language, and she would never utter a coarse joke. Unfortunately, there are many women today who talk more loudly and are more boisterous than any man would dare to be. As a young girl, you must learn now to always master your emotions regarding your voice. Do not shout, rage, or whine. You really do want to be someone that others gravitate to, not run away from. Keeping control of your tongue is so very important. Ask God daily to help you.

****

Discussion:

~Take the time to imitate the following ways that a man would:
1. Walk; 2. Sit; 3. Talk

~Discuss how a young lady should sit, walk and talk.

1 Timothy 2:9 tells us: "In like manner also, that women adorn themselves in modest apparel, with shamefacedness and sobriety..."

~According to scripture, are women to be loud, in either clothing or voice level?
~What does shamefacedness mean to you? (According to the Strong's Concordance, shamefacedness means, "Downcast eyes, bashfulness towards men, modesty, awe towards God, or reverence.")
~What does sobriety mean to you? (Sobriety means, "soundness of mind, sanity, self-control.")
~Explain how "self-control" is involved with femininity in our move ments, our manners and our speech.
~Is it easy to be feminine?
~Name some areas that you know you might have to work on.
~Sit down and write these out on a piece of paper and then take them to the Lord in prayer. Talk to God about all of your shortcom ings and ask Him to help you be an overcomer in these areas.
~Keep a daily journal on how you have failed in certain areas and how you have overcome. This will help you to remember these things and to not forget what you are trying to do. Read over your journal each week of what you have written previously.
~Keep your thoughts on becoming a feminine Christian woman whose sole desire is to be pleasing to her Maker!

Chapter Four

WHICH WAY WILL YOU CHOOSE?

Dearest sister, you have a choice in which type of woman you will become. There are many choices to choose from. You can choose to follow the world and its ways and become a woman of the world. You can choose to follow the entertainment industry and try to copy fiction, that is, those actresses on the screens whose lives are not real. Or, you can choose to follow God and try to be a woman pleasing to Him.

Would God want you to be a feminine woman? He would have you be content in who you are, because this is what He intended.

One part of becoming more feminine is learning to depend on those stronger than you. This is what we are going to discuss in this chapter. The art of being willing to *not dominate* and *to depend on the males* in our lives. This is something that has not been taught in this century. You may be told that this is outdated and old, but then these same whisperers would say the same about our precious Scriptures. The Scriptures are not outdated or old, and they is where this thought comes from. Straight from the Word of God!

Refusing to Dominate

Have you ever seen a dominating woman? This creature is far more terrifying than any insect you might find. She is a person who is very controlling of others. The dictionary tells us that a dominating person overlooks from a great height. She is lofty and prideful, assuming that her way is better than others and that all other's ways are wrong.

A dominating girl will become a dominating woman, so it is so important that if you have any of these tendencies, that you bring them to our Savior and repent as we speak. Otherwise, it will only become worse over time.

Why is it so bad that a female be dominant? Because this is breaking God's rules. He has created men, from the beginning of the Book, to be the dominant personality in the relationship between a male and female. When a woman usurps that authority and starts to control her family rather than her husband, anarchy exists and this terrible state can ruin future generations.

Do you find yourself wanting to be in control? Are you wanting your way above that of your parents or your brothers and sisters? Be very careful that you quell this in your personality and take it to God. He can help you overcome this now. He can help even those with a terribly controlling personality, if you will seek Him.

Willing to be Dependent on Others

God has created women to become wives, mothers and homemakers. But do you realize that each of these things takes something to make them so? Can a young lady by herself be a wife? A mother? A homemaker? No. What does it take to become each of these things? It takes another. It took Adam to make Eve.

From the very beginning of time, God created females to be dependent upon the males. Just as males receive great satisfaction from being needed and dependent upon, so were females to receive joy in being dependent upon males. And God made males to give their protection and provision with great satisfaction. It is part of their make up to take care of women.

The Lord created females to help the males. "And the Lord God said, It is not good that the man should be alone. I will make him an help meet for him." Genesis 2:18

We are the male's "helpers". They are not our helpers. We were not created for them, but rather females were created for the males. Eve was not created first, Adam was.

What does this mean regarding being dependent upon the men in our lives? It is in developing a heart attitude of willing to be weaker. We need to be willing to be dependent, otherwise we "demand" and make feminine, the men in our lives.

Developing a Submissive Will

God created men to be our protectors. We are to look to them as our protectors and providers. When we look at the men in our lives in this way, they will look at us as those needing to be protected and cared for.

A girl who refuses to have a submissive will has the opposite... a rebellious will.

The scriptures talk an awful lot about rebellion and rebelliousness.

"Woe to the rebellious children, saith the Lord, that take counsel, but not of me; and that cover with a covering, but not of my spirit, that they may add sin to sin." Isaiah 30:1

God tells us that we are not to listen to the ways of the world, but we are to take counsel (or teaching) from Him only. When we listen to people who tell us that we are not to submit to our fathers or husbands, we are adding sin to sin.

"That this is a rebellious people, lying children, children that will not hear the law of the Lord." Isaiah 30:9

We must learn now to obey the Scriptures. If we do not, then we will become rebellious. A rebellious girl will make a rebellious wife. Pity the poor man who has a woman who will not submit to him; but, who must live all his life in misery because of her rebelliousness.

"...because she hath been rebellious against me, saith the Lord. Thy way and thy doings have procured these things unto thee; this is thy wickedness, because it is bitter, because it reacheth unto thine heart." Jeremiah 4:17-18

When we refuse to submit to our parent's will, we will only reap sorrow unto ourselves. Now is the time to start having an obedient heart to the authority in your own family. First, God and His Word. Second, your father, who is the head of your family. Third, your mother, who is in authority when your father is absent from the home.

"But this people hath a revolting and a rebellious heart; they are revolted and gone. Neither say they in their heart, Let us now fear the Lord our God, that giveth rain, both the former and the latter, in His season; He reserveth unto us the appointed weeks of the harvest. Your iniquities have turned away these things, ***and your sins have withholden good things from you.****" Jeremiah 5:23-25*

Did you know that you withhold good things from happening to you when you walk in disobedience? When you do not submit to the authority of whom God has placed over you, (your father, your mother and eventually your husband), you will only hurt yourself!

The Scriptures tell women, "Wives, submit yourselves unto your own husbands." Ephesians 5:22 & Colossians 3:18

Dearest sister in Christ, it is of the utmost importance that you learn now how to submit your will to that of others. Do you know what this really means? Let me give you an example:

There was a young lady whose parents had told her that she was not allowed to go to the dance hall because they didn't believe that she should ever try to meet young men at such a place as this. The parents only believed in family members or close friends introducing eligible young men to her.

The daughter didn't think that her parents were capable of choosing a young man for her and so, willfully, decided she could do better by herself.

She lied to her parents and went out to the dance hall one night, where people were drinking and partying, and there she met a young man. She continued having a relationship with him, keeping this secret from her parents. The two of them eventually went off and eloped (got married without their parent's permission).

But this disobedience and rebelliousness only hurt herself, for after two years of marriage, the young man was found unfaithful. He also was a terrible drinker of liquor, and would get into a rage and beat her.

Her willful rebelliousness caused her a lifetime of pain and misery because she refused to submit to the will of her loving parents. These parents had told her not to go to the dance hall simply because they cared about her and knew that she would not find a suitable husband in a place like that. This is about being willing to submit your will to that of your parent's.

You must give your will over to those who are older and wiser in Christ. First, this starts with your family as you are a young girl. Next, you must submit to your husband.

Being Capable But Not Independent

Many women in the world think that being submissive means that a woman cannot be capable. They are so very wrong! The Proverbs 31 woman is a description of one that is very capable of running a household. The heart of her husband trusts in her to be able to do her duties!

How wonderful it is to find a wife that has the ability for action, and is efficient, regarding the home and the raising of children! In order to become capable, you must be able to learn household duties as a young girl. This way, you will be ready for anything that comes your way.

But being capable doesn't mean that we are to be "independent". Our society teaches young girls that their main goal is to be independent of others, especially males. They are not ever taught that it is actually a good thing to be dependent upon a man.

Being independent will not make you admirable to anyone.

Your parents will not find you charming at all if you are just listening to your own thoughts and not considering all those around you. Your husband, in the future, will not find you anyone whom he would be able to "care for" and to protect and provide for throughout the rest of your life. Who needs to care for someone who is "independent"? This attitude is one that is based in pride. Again, something that God does not wish His daughters to exude.

Do you overpower other people? This is not a feminine trait. This is something that most men do. Take a good look at yourself. Do you demand to do things by yourself, or do you ask others if you can do things for them? There is a difference.

The *independent* girl will usually only do things that will better herself. She is innately selfish. That is what independence brings when it concerns females. Even when it seems she is helping others it is simply because she wants to do something that makes "her" feel good. A self-righteous type of helping.

On the other hand, the *dependent* girl will look around her and see the needs of those she loves. She does things, not from an independent spirit, but from one who sees that everyone works together and gives. The dependent girl is one who does everything with the motivation of contributing with others to achieve one whole. This is also like the example the scriptures give us concerning the body of Christ.

****

Discussion:

~What does the word *submissive* mean? (It means being willing to be obedient to others who are in authority. This

means being willing to listen and obey our Heavenly Father, our earthly dad, our mother. The dictionary definition means: "obedience, yielding or surrendering oneself to the will or authority of another. Compliant, meekness.")
~Can you think of ways in which you are submissive to your family?
~Can you think of ways in which you are not?
~How are we to be capable but not independent?
~Give an example.
~Do you know the definition of independent? (Free from the influence, guidance, or control of another or others; self-reliant. Self-supporting.)
~Compare the definitions of *submissive* to *independent.*
~Are they opposites?
~Describe how and why.

Read: Proverbs 1:5
~How is an independent spirit against God? (It is against God because we are all dependent 100% on our Heavenly Father. To be independent states that you are relying only on self. This is opposite to what God says we should be. We are to obey and trust God first, and then His authority structure, God, Jesus, Man, Wife then children.)

Read: "Then Peter and the other apostles answered and said, 'We ought to obey God rather than men.'"Acts 5:29

~When we are independent rather than dependent on God and His ways, who are we obeying?

Read: "That they may teach the younger women to... be dis creet, chaste, keepers at home, good, *obedient to their own husbands*, that the Word of God be not blasphemed." Titus 2:5

Discuss this scripture at length regarding submission.

Chapter Five

HOW DOES A FEMININE GIRL SPEAK?

Speaking Gently

How we speak is also a very important aspect of our feminity.

Have you ever been surprised to hear a loud, obnoxious bellow and turn to see it coming out of a tiny, little girl? Or a lovely on the outside, type of older girl?

What happens? I know that I am usually a bit shocked. For where only softly spoken words should be coming out of a girl who is trying to live for Christ, harsh, loud words are there instead.

Why is this so important? One reason is that this ruins your example of femininity. Think of how you feel when you are being told something loudly. How does this make you feel? You might not be able to listen to what the person is saying. You are only responding to the WAY it is being said. This is very important.

When your sister or brother speaks loudly to you, do you respond with love and kindness in your heart? Or do you tend to get a bit perturbed at being yelled at.

God would have us speak gently. We are to be gentle.

The scriptures tell us:

"Flee also youthful lusts; but follow righteousness, faith, charity, peace, with them that call on the Lord out of a pure heart. But foolish and unlearned questions avoid, knowing that they do gender strifes. ***And the servant of the Lord must not strive; but be gentle unto all men..."*** *2 Timothy 2:22-24*

To be gentle means to speak things so that they are received graciously by those that hear you. When you speak gently, it will give peace to those who listen.

"A soft answer turns away wrath." Proverbs 15:1

"By long suffering is a prince persuaded, and a soft tongue breaketh the bone." Proverbs 25:15

These scriptures are telling us why we need to speak gently. There is much power in gentleness, even though the world will tell you differently. The world might believe that the pushier you are the more you will get. But God's Word tells us the opposite.

Remember to speak gently with everyone you meet. Even when you are angry, be a peacemaker! Put God above self.

Speaking With Humility

What do you think it means to "speak with humility?" What would the opposite of humility be? Pride. That's right.

What is a "know-it-all"? Unfortunately, all of us have a tendency to want to be right. But, a serious problem some women have is that of wanting to know-it-all. This is a reaction of pride.

The scriptures tell us that God does not like pride at all.

"These six things doth the Lord hate; yea, seven are an abomination unto him. ***A proud look..."*** *Proverbs 6:16-17*

The scriptures taught about a person having a haughty or proud look. Disdainful. Like when a girl chooses to look down her nose at another human being. God HATES this. We are to truly consider all men higher than ourselves, otherwise we become an abomination to God.

"Every one that is proud in heart is an abomination to the Lord; though hand join in hand, he shall not be unpunished." Proverbs 16:5

Not only are we not to look down upon others, we are not to have pride in our hearts. When we allow pride to come into our hearts, we have not allowed God to be King. We let ourselves then become God.

"Whoso keepeth his mouth and his tongue keepeth his soul from troubles. Proud and haughty scorner is his name, who dealeth in proud wrath." Proverbs 21:23-24

Think about this scripture. What happens when we can keep (or control) our mouths and our tongues? The Bible says that it will keep our very soul from troubles. When we speak haughtily or with pride, we scorn the very Lord that we claim.

"Wherefore he saith, 'God resisteth the proud, but giveth grace unto the humble.' Submit yourselves therefore to God. Resist the devil and he will flee from you." James 4:6

Everything that we say should be spoken in humility. Remember that God Himself will resist you if you are speaking arrogantly or pridefully.

For example, when you are dealing with your family members, do you ever shout at them to come and do something that they are supposed to be doing? Wouldn't you get more of a response if you humbly ask them in a quiet tone to come and help? If they see that you are not arrogant or bossy, won't they be more likely to respond in a similar manner?

Never Using Ugly Expressions

What is in your heart is what you will speak.

*"**But those things which proceed out of the mouth come forth from the heart; and they defile the man**. For out of the heart proceed evil thoughts, murders, adulteries, fornications, thefts, false witness, blasphemies, these are the things that defile a man; but to eat with unwashen hands defileth not a man." Matthew 15:18*

God doesn't want his feminine creation to speak coarsely! (Nor his male creation for that matter). Can you imagine a beautiful girl, poised, composed in her dress and manner, and then from her open mouth comes awful words of anger and hatred? This is a terrible picture!

A young girl must remember to never say anything ugly. No ugly words or sentences whatsoever.

"Let no corrupt communication proceed out of your mouth, but that which is good to the use of edifying, that it may minister grace unto the hearers." Ephesians 4:29

This doesn't mean just bad words. This is also true regarding poisonous words.

What are poisonous words? Things that poison others who hear you talking.

For example, if you are talking about your brother being unkind to you, you will poison the other person, your friend, for instance, to take a dislike to your brother. This is because she will like you and not want others to be mean to you, so if she hears you saying how awful your brother is treating you, she will no longer look at your brother in a kind way. You have then poisoned your friend, AND your brother. You have hurt and betrayed them both.

Another example is saying you don't like something. By your

saying that you don't like something or some one, you poison other people from liking the same object.

The point of the matter is to always keep poisonous thoughts and poisonous words to yourself.

Speak only things which would bring life and happiness and encouragement to other people. Make that a top goal in your life and you will always find joy and happiness all around you, rather than gloom and criticism!

Speaking Honestly

When you are speaking, always speak honestly. For example, if a friend asks you to do something that you know you are not to do, simply say, "I do not want to."

This is honest. This is direct. This will keep you out of trouble!

This type of speaking will not hurt the person you are talking to, and you do not have to make excuses. It is being direct and open, but spoken gently.

If your grandmother takes you shopping and wishes to buy you something that you do not like, it would be honest to tell her. You could say, "I don't really like that one, Grandmother. Would it be all right to get something different?"

That is much better. It keeps your heart pure.

When talking with people, do not hint. That is not being honest, and most of the time, people will not get your hint. Be up front and open.

Learning to Stop Gossip Kindly

Some women have a difficult time with gossip, or talking negatively about others.

An example would be, when two girls are talking among themselves about another girl who is not there with them. Remember, do not be talking about friends when they are not around. This hurts them. This is unkind, and God's feminine girl does not wish to be unkind.

Did you know one of the Ten Commandments is about "gossip"?

"Thou shalt not bear false witness against thy neighbor."

The scriptures call a gossip a "TALEBEARER". It's bearing tales about other people.

"The words of a talebearer are as wounds, and they go down into the innermost parts of the belly." Proverbs 18:8

"Where no wood is, there the fire goeth out; so where there is no talebearer, the strife ceaseth. As coals are to burning coals, and wood to fire; so is a contentious man to kindle strife. The words of a talebearer are as wounds and go down into the innermost parts of the belly." Proverbs 26:20-22

Gossip is the result of an unforgiving heart. We talk about others when we are unforgiving of their faults. We need to cultivate a forgiving heart.

God does not want us to "get even" with people whom we think have hurt us or deserve it. Jesus taught us that we should never pay back "evil for evil" but to turn the other cheek.

Gossip needs to be put to death and instead we need to cultivate a loving and forgiving character. Even the worst person on earth can change through the power of our living God and through His son, Jesus Christ.

If someone else is gossiping and you do not wish to follow along, simply remember to be honest and say, "I'm really trying to keep my heart pure regarding this person and don't really wish to talk about this. Thank you."

****

Discussion:

~What does "speaking gently" mean to you?

~How will you exercise speaking gently?
~Does this mean that you can never yell?

~God talks about speaking in humility. If you come across a discussion in which you are participating, and the people are arguing with you and saying things that are unbiblical, how will you respond?
~If someone is talking about women being the head of their homes, for instance. How would you respond?
~Give an example of how you would respond know-it-all-ish and then humbly.

~What does the Bible say about speaking coarsely?
~Why is this not feminine?
~How would a feminine girl try to always speak?

~Have you ever gossiped?
~Did you feel better after having done so, or did you feel its poison in your heart?
~How can you kindly change the subject if someone is gos siping?
~How is not gossiping being honest?

"But the younger widows refuse... And withal they learn to be idle, wandering about from house to house; and not only idle, but tattlers also and busybodies, speaking things which they ought not." 1 Timothy 5:13

~What goes along with being a tattler and busybody? (Being idle)
~Why would being "idle" have anything to do with being a tattler and a busybody? (Because if they were busy, they wouldn't have time to sit and talk about other people, but would mind their own business.)

Chapter Six

A FEMININE CHRISTIAN CHARACTER

Character Is The Most Important Thing

"Reputation is who people *think* you are. Character *is what you truly* are."

You can put on faces for different people, but this doesn't really mean that this is who you are. You can pretend to be someone for a period of time, but if you aren't really who you are pretending to be, you will soon be found out.

Did you know that your character is continuously changing? This is true! Have you ever looked at a young child who is four and then not see them for a while? Then you may come across them two or three years later. What has happened? They have changed tremendously, of course!

This is what happens with each of us. Our character is continuously in formation.

If you are a Christian, God is perfecting you for Him. He tells us that He will be doing this throughout our whole lives.

"Be sober, be vigilant; because your adversary the devil, as a roaring lion, walketh about, seeking whom he may devour; whom resist steadfast in the faith, knowing that the same afflictions are accomplished in your brethren that are in the world. But the God of all grace, who hath called us unto his eternal glory by Christ Jesus, after that ye have suffered a while, make you perfect, establish, strengthen, settle you." 1 Peter 5:8-10

This is so very comforting! God will perfect us! But we must be willing to be perfected. We must want to change into someone who has a character that reflects our love of God.

To have good character would be to have a character that would want to do good. I'm sure that you do not wish to do bad or to do evil. Most of us don't. It is when choices come up in life that makes us choose to do good or to not do good. It's that simple. Hopefully, with the power of God's Spirit, you will be able to make good choices for Him all throughout your life.

Did you know that all of life is a test? It is to try us and test us to make us better for God.

For example, if you were locked in a bubble with a Bible, you could read the Bible all you wanted, but you would never be able to go out of that bubble and actually DO or LIVE anything that you have read. If you had no interaction with others in this world, you would never have a time to try out what you actually believed. Do you understand this?

Did you know that if you only *pretend* to have a good character you are deceitful? Good character comes from loving God and choosing each day to serve Him!

Learning to Have Modesty and Keeping Chaste

Did you know that modesty is one of the most beautiful traits of Christian femininity? It is a character trait that comes from within. We talked a bit previously about this regarding clothing, but now we must take it a bit deeper.

God would have us as womanhood be pure in heart. In being modest it is absolutely opposite what the world teaches young girls. For example, the world will tell us that being a loud mouth, demanding and bossy is fine. But, no, this is not fine. This is not modest. Calling attention to oneself in any way, is not fine.

You may have seen young girls that you know dressing in order to attract boys. This is not a pure and modest heart. Boys will only look upon girls that have hearts like this for entertainment purposes. In most instances, boys who respond to such girls will probably not be following God.

This brings us to some very important information regarding modesty and chastity...

In our world, we have seen a new trend of young teenagers having babies with their boyfriends, and refusing to get married. This is called fornication, and the scriptures forbid this.

*"**Flee fornication**. Every sin that a man doeth is without the body; but he that committeth fornication sinneth against his own body. What? **Know ye not that your body is the temple of the Holy Ghost** which is in you, which ye have of God, and ye are not your own? For ye are bought with a price; therefore glorify God in your body, and in your spirit, which are God's." 1 Corinthians 6:18; Galatians 5:19; Ephesians 5:3*

The scriptures here are so very clear. As young girls, you must keep your bodies pure and always remember that your body is the temple of the Holy Ghost. This is God's Word, not man's word.

In our day, we find that being chaste is not important to people who do not love God. They believe that you can have many different people to love. But God's Word teaches that there is only one man for you to marry, and you will marry for life. To break His Word only brings unhappiness and sorrow.

Girls and women who have a chaste character are the ones who will bring up children who are chaste and love God. Their lives are full and they are content because they have done things God's way.

You must be morally clean.

To engage in fornication makes you *morally unclean*, and then you will no longer have a character that is pleasing to God. You will become hardened to the voice of God and to His Word. You will become carnal and fleshly, which the Scriptures say is absolutely terrible!

The consequences of not following God ruin your life. Breaking these laws of God causes moral problems not only for yourself, but for future generations. When our society rejected the moral beliefs of God's Word in this area of chastity, we became a society of carnality. The flesh rules these people, and they have absolutely nothing in the area of modesty to pass on to their children.

When a girl or woman is morally pure she has something that no amount of makeup or hair styles can give her. She has a look of innocence about her. This is where true beauty lies. When a girl is unclean morally her very looks change and she starts to harden and to become ugly, both on the outside, and on the inside.

Another consequence of this terrible sin is that it ruins the girl's character. She becomes corrupt and will corrupt all those around her. They then become deceivers and live in rebellion towards God.

"For to be carnally minded is death; but to be spiritually minded is life and peace. Because the carnal mind is enmity against God; for it is not subject to the law of God, neither indeed can be. So then they that are in the flesh cannot please God." Romans 8:6-8

If and when you find that you are in a position where you are ready to get married, and you find a young man who is interested in you, it is very important that you make sure that your first kiss is on your wedding day when the pastor says, "Now you may kiss the bride."

Regardless of what you may have heard, kissing is only for marriage. To do so without marriage is very, very foolish. Why should a young man marry a girl, if she kisses him without the benefit of being married to him?

Marriage is a protection for women. They are to be protected and cared for and honored in marriage.

If you have "boyfriends" as the world tells us, and you break God's way of doing things, a girl would set herself up to be a "passing toy", to be discarded when he loses interest. The girl then will have nothing but sorrow and dishonor in the eyes of God.

You may see things in movies or on television that tell you other ways, but these ways are unclean and are not of our Heavenly Father. God will give you a wonderful life and your marriage will be truly blessed by Him, if you wait until that day for any type of physical intimacy.

Do not allow anyone to ever tell you anything differently. If someone tries to dissuade you or discourage you in keeping yourself pure, immediately tell your mother or your father so that they can help you.

Watch out for familiar pats on the backs by any male who is not in your family. Do not allow them to touch you in any way.

Did you know that being "chaste" means morally pure, decent; modest; untouched?

Isn't that lovely? And that is what you will be, lovely, when you follow the instructions God has given us in His book!

Charity & Goodwill

Genuine Christian femininity has a character of true concern for other people. She has a heart that truly loves and wants to help all those with whom she is involved.

She will love and be thoughtful of her parents. Do you ever think about your mother? How your mother loves and cares for you, and how her life might be? Do you ever think how hard she works to take care of you and your family?

If you haven't really given it much thought, start having concern for her. If she has heavy duties to bear, and you haven't ever looked around the house for ways you can help, start doing so. This is how you change and develop thoughtfulness for everyone else. It starts in your very own home. If you are not thoughtful at home, how will you be thoughtful elsewhere.

Do you ever overlook people who are around you simply because they are quiet? How about at church or at school functions? Do you ever see older people who are in the background? Have a heart for them. Take time to talk to them and show a caring character. If you do not have this in your heart, you can develop this. You can change your character, remember. God helps us to change everyday!

Having a Gracious & Forgiving Heart

This is one of the most important character traits that a person can develop throughout her life.

You will find that there will be many times that people will hurt you or offend you.

"Be ye kind one to another, tenderhearted, forgiving one another, even as God for Christ's sake hath forgiven you." Ephesians 4:32

Many people take that hurt and want to hurt back. But God doesn't tell us to do this. Jesus told us if someone slapped us on one cheek, to turn the other and let him slap that one too. We aren't to want to "get anyone back" in any way!

"17. Recompense to no man evil for evil. ... 19. Avenge not yourselves, but rather give place unto wrath; for it is written 'Vengeance is mine; I will repay, saith the Lord... 21. ***Be not overcome of evil, but overcome evil with good****." Romans 12*

If you have a good character in the eyes of God, you will be forgiving. You must be able to rise above your own feelings and emotion and to do what God tells us to do. Sometimes it is not easy when you are wounded. But God heals our wounds. He heals our hearts. He "heals the brokenhearted", His Word tells us.

When we have been hurt by others, or when we see terrible flaws in others, we must remember that we, too, have flaws.

"Do unto others as you would have them do unto you."

The Golden Rule...

Have you ever been thoughtlessly unkind to someone but haven't realized it at the time? If you look back over actions where you have unknowingly hurt a friend, wouldn't it have been awful if they hadn't overlooked your actions? You might be devastated to find out all the wrong things you have done unknowingly. But, hopefully, your friends and family members are gracious and kind, and overlook your negative side.

When you do not forgive, you only hurt yourself. You are the only one who is going to be harmed in the long run. The scriptures say that we will even harm ourselves by unforgiveness.

"Let all bitterness, and wrath, and anger, and clamor, and evil speaking, be put away from you, and all malice; and be ye kind one to another, tenderhearted, forgiving one another, even as God for Christ's sake hath forgiven you." Ephesians 4:31

Bitterness is what happens to a person who won't forgive. Have you ever seen a bitter person? They see everything through a negative, unkind, spiteful eye. They usually have nothing good to say about anything or any one.

Forgive your enemies. Love your enemies. Do good to those that hate you. This is the way of God. And with this way comes joy.

Being Humble

What does it mean to be humble? If you think you are humble you probably are not. Being humble means that you show humility rather than pride. It means that you are aware of your shortcomings; modest (again!); meek. It means that you do not put on airs, but that you are unpretentious.

Some people think that you must have a "low" view of yourself, but this isn't an exact description of humility. You don't look down on yourself, but you also don't elevate yourself. You just be content with being a creature of God, a sinner who has been saved by grace, and live each day, hoping to better ourselves in Christ!

Being truly humble is one of the most important characteristics that a person can have.

The opposite isn't a very pretty picture. It would portray a girl or woman who is prideful regarding her home, her clothes, or family, her accomplishments, her talents... It goes on and on.

As we have learned previously, the Scriptures tell us that God *hates* pride. It is an abomination to Him. He can't look at us with attitudes such as this.

One thing that many well meaning Christian's unfortunately portray is self-righteousness. They might have a tendency to view themselves as better than others because of their following God.

We must remember to never compare ourselves with others and think we are better than they are. When we do this with other people who are not behaving as they should, we then become terribly Pharisaic. Remember the scripture of the tax collector who fell on his face before God and the religious man looking upon Him praying, "Dear God, thank you that I am not such as HE..."?

One thing to ALWAYS remember, there is hope for every single person on the face of this earth in the eyes of God, as long as they live. We must remember that they can change, and you do not know what God may do with them in the future. In this is your humility.

Last, but not least, remember, no matter how "good" you may think you are, there is always someone better... And at the end of that line is perfection, the Lord Jesus!!!!

Being Virtuous
(Being Bold Enough to Live What You believe)

Did you know that one of the attributes of virtue is to be bold in what you believe? Being virtuous not only means to be kept pure in the eyes of God by doing what He would have you do, but it also means being willing to actually DO what he would have you do. In the face of adversity, for example, with all your friends making fun of you and doing exactly the opposite, you going ahead and doing what you know is right, is virtue!

Are there some things that you know are right and true; but, you may find it difficult to live out? I know that many dear friends will believe something that God has shown them in their heads, but it hasn't yet reached their heart for them to live it out.

Virtue is believing something and then having the courage to do it!

One thing that might be difficult to do, is to truly live out being a feminine Christian girl in the face of feminism today. Many young girls have been taught that there is no difference between being a boy and being a girl. This is not true. There are great differences in how we look, how we speak, what we are to do, our duties, that are all listed in the Word of God.

But many people have bought the lie of feminism and do not yet have their minds renewed to what His Word says to us about this. This is where true courage or virtue come in. The ability to believe God more than what anyone else might say, and follow through and DO what He says.

"But be ye doers of the word, and not hearers only, deceiving your own selves, for if any be a hearer of the word, and not a doer, he is like unto a man beholding his natural face in a glass; for he beholdeth himself, and goeth his way, and straightway forgetteth what manner of man he was." James 1:22-24

Being virtuous means being a DOER of the Word of God. You must read the Scriptures and then go DO what it says!

The Value of Unselfishness

What does it mean to you to be unselfish? Think about this for a moment. Well, a selfish person is a person who thinks only about their own comforts and does things only if they "get something out of it". It is a person who puts their self first, before any one else.

You must learn the art of being unselfish. The first way to do this is by sharing. It is of thinking of others before you think of yourself.

I once heard a very good analogy of what unselfishness is. It was that a young girl once had a book that she treasured more than any of her other books. It was about God and she could read it and learn more about Him. One day a friend came to her and told her that she didn't have any books to read. The girl looked around her room and saw many books that her parents had given her. But then her eye fell on her most precious treasure, THE BOOK. She hated to part with it for she loved this book, but it was her very best book, and if she was going to be giving her friend a book, she wanted her to have the very best. So she went over and gently picked up THE BOOK and gave it to her.

This is what unselfishness is. It is to be able to truly give that which matters at the sacrifice of self. Not the other way around. To make sure that oneself benefits always, and to puts others second. This is selfishness.

When a girl or woman is unselfish, she is becoming more beautiful with every year that passes by. For she has learned to attain true beauty of the heart!

****

DISCUSSION:

~Why is character the most important thing?
~What's the difference between reputation and character?

~How can you develop Godly character?
~Why is it important to have modesty?
~What does it mean to you to be chaste?
~If you found yourself in a situation where a young man was making you uncomfortable by trying to become too familiar, what would you do?
~Why is it important to wait until marriage to receive your first kiss?
~What Scriptures back this up? (1 Corinthians 6:18; Galatians ~5:19; Ephesians 5:3)
~What does the Bible say about being carnally minded? (Ro mans 8:6-8 tells us that to be carnally minded is death.)
~Does this mean physical death? (No, spiritual. But many times in our day, it also brings physical death because of the diseases of impurity.)
~What does it mean to you to have true charity and goodwill towards others?
~How can you be more thoughtful towards others?
~Why is it important that you are forgiving?
~What happens to you if you aren't forgiving? (You will be come bitter or full of bitterness.)
~What happens to a person with bitterness? (Their outlook on life becomes an ugly one. Everything in God's world will become ugly and negative to them. They will be unhappy forever.)
~Are we to take revenge when people wrong us or hurt us? (The Bible tells us that we are not to repay any man evil for evil. We are to overcome evil with good. Romans 12:21)
~What is humility or being humble?
~How does being virtuous affect your walk in life?
~What does being truly virtuous mean?
~Are you a hearer or a doer?
~What would God have you be?
~Describe how you can be better in DOING the Word of God in your life...

Chapter Seven

TAKING CARE OF GOD'S TEMPLE, YOUR PHYSICAL FORM

Your Body is God's Temple

Have you ever thought about how very blessed by God you are that you have such a wonderful body that functions so perfectly? God made you just as you are.

In the Bible, our bodies are called a "temple". A temple, you know in the Old Testament, was a place where God resided or lived. Did you know that your body is a temple where the Holy Spirit lives? Can you imagine how sacred the temple of old was? When they entered the temple of God they behaved as if they were before the Living God and were on their best behavior.

But even that building was made by men's hands. Our body is made by the hand of the great Creator and is, therefore, much more sacred than even the man-made temple.

We then ought to be so very thankful to God for His creation and take care of it with reverence. Reverence means with love and affection and thankfulness. We must think of our bodies as sacred and to reverence them because they are created by God; and, because we were of so much importance that Christ died for us.

Can you imagine a princess and how she would wear beautiful clothes and be so very beautiful in heart and spirit and form? But did you know that you, dear sister in Christ, are the daughter of the King of Kings? Your clothing should be more beautiful than those of any princess on earth. And you are! You are beautifully clothed in the body that God created.

See, you are not your body. The real you is inside your body, and your body is your dress, the clothing that your Heavenly Father has made for you. This dress, your earthly form, has been made beautiful by God's Divine Hand and it is cared for and kept in repair by His Power.

If we could see the body through a microscope, we would see that it's made of small atoms, called cells, and each one of these cells has a certain time to live.

God has made us so that our bodies are kept in repair by the food that we eat. It is taken into the stomach and made over into a fluid, which is carried into our blood vessels, and becoming blood, is taken to every organ in your body.

If you eat the right types of food, your blood will have all that it needs for healthy bones, muscles, nerves and all that God has created your "dress" with.

Why do we get "out of repair"? Because we are continually active. You run and play. You work and think and all of these activities use up some part of the material that our bodies are made of. New material must be replaced to take the place of that which has been destroyed.

If all the activities of your body are destroying some part of its substance, what becomes of this dead material? It is being cast out through various organs of your body. Through the bowels a quantity of solid waste matter is cast out; through the bladder, fluid waste matter, and a large quantity of waste material passes out invisibly through the lungs and through the skin. You might be surprised to know that a larger part passes out through your skin in a twenty-four hour period than through the bowels.

This shows the need to bathe often, for the surface of the body is covered with little pores, or mouths, and these need to be kept open in order that we shall be healthy.

If the material which passes out is allowed to accumulate on the surface of the body, it closes up these little mouths and people do not feel well.

When you bathe, it is a wonderful thing to have a loofah mitt, or some type of bathing brush to brush your skin. Did you know that this is what people have used for thousands of years? Why? Because they knew this truth!

So do you understand the importance of keeping your body clean? Just as we clean our houses every day in order to keep it picked up and livable, so do we need to clean our bodily dwellings or homes, very often also!

Eating For Health, Not for Pleasure

Just as we need to keep the outside of our "temple" clean, we also need to take good care of the inside. You do this through watching what you put in your body.

Many people believe that milk, eggs, oatmeal, entire wheat flour and fruits and vegetables are the best foods in order to make strong bones, nerves and muscles. You would do well to always remember to eat light protein, fresh vegetables and fruits, whole grains and nuts. But *not* to overeat!

Girls or young women who are eating sweets and indigestible substances will find that they are not as healthy as they could be. They would be much more energetic, and would protect their bodies for their old age, if they ate only simple, nourishing food regularly.

We need to also remember to drink wholesome drinks. Water is the only natural drink, and pure water is the best fluid to take into the system. In fruits, we take fluids in a very pleasant way, and milk is also full of water. From these three sources we can obtain as much water as our temples need.

Tea and coffee have been proven to be very bad for us. Especially young women. They make people feel that they have had something to eat, when in reality they have given no nourishment to the body at all!

Coffee and tea are stimulants. A stimulant creates an appearance of strength, without really giving strength. Children need nourishing food to build up new material as well as to keep the body in repair, and if they take into the body poisons, they will harm their God-given rebuilding process.

Researchers tell us that the reason caffeine stimulates our bodies is because it is a poison and our systems react frantically to rid our bodies of this poison, which is why it is called a "stimulant"?

Something for you to really think upon, dear sister, is not forming habits when you are so young. This is another thing about addictive eating patterns. It seems so important that we are not a slave to our flesh and our lusts or wants. It is far more nobler to master your body than to be mastered by it. It is a wise girl who will not allow herself to form a habit that will make her in any way a slave.

You need to grow up a free woman, free from all habits that are wrong, from everything that fetters and chains you. You need to be free to think, free to act, and free to serve God with every faculty of your mind and body. You must not use anything that will prevent your thinking clearly, or use anything that will dull your judgment or your moral sense or make you in any way a less godly, noble woman than God designed you to be.

"But I keep under my body, and bring it into subjection; lest that by any means, when I have preached to others, I myself should be a castaway." 1 Corinthians 9:27

Learning Good Nutrition & How to Feed Your Future Family

What is good nutrition? It is putting into your temple only things that are good nutrients or nutritional food. We talked a little bit before about certain foods which we should put in our body, and a little about what we should not.

Do not trust your appetite! Your appetite is so very deceiving! We may think that french fries, candy canes, chocolates, ice cream sundaes, sugar coated cereal, are good. They may taste good, all right, but are they good for your body, the temple of the Holy Ghost? No, they are not. This doesn't mean that you may not indulge yourself once in a while. But you must not make your diet always consist of these types of food.

If you learn now how to eat properly, you will then make a wonderful wife and mother. Remember, you are not only going to be living for yourself all your life. You are a servant of God, and your future holds wonderful adventures waiting for you! Most probably, that of marriage and motherhood! So, when you are learning how to eat properly for yourself, you are also learning how to feed your own children.

There are so many foods on the grocery shelves. What choices we have today! But we need to learn to make the *right* choices!

The best rule of eating:

EAT THINGS THAT GOD HAS MADE, NOT MAN.

Can mankind make a grape, or a tomato, or a pineapple? No! And they cannot copy it, either, though they do try. Remember to always try to buy food that God has created, not what man has processed. We can then take that food and turn it into nutritious meals.

Another thing to remember is to buy food when it is in season. Did you know that winter squash is called that because it lasts all winter?

In the past, people had "root cellars". Many of the food that they purchased or grew in the fall would last them all winter if it was stored properly in the root cellar. Grains remain fresh for several seasons.

Stay away from processed and refined foods. They contain preservatives which are not good for our bodies. They also are missing nutrients and so they are puffed back up with "fake" vitamins that are man-made.

Again, drink plenty of fluids in order to keep your cells lush and able to grow.

You must also remember to exercise your body; God's temple. Do not sit idle. Walking is a wonderful way to exercise, and you can walk even when you are old!

Weight Control

We have just discussed the issue of being a slave to anything on this earth. This also includes the sin of overeating. A weight problem stems from the fact that we are not able to bring our appetites under control. If we give our temples too much food, fat will stick to our muscles. This is not good. It can hurt your heart, your lungs, and clog your blood vessels.

But skinny people can also have an eating problem. They may not eat foods that are good for them and so might look thin, but they are hurting their bodies. They will suffer in their old age.

God would have us bring all things to the cross. The perfect diet is to eat to keep your body alive. Not to live to eat. There is a huge difference.

You do not have to look like the girl on the front of a magazine displayed for you at the grocery store! Our bodies weren't meant to be paper thin, especially since you will be having babies in your future. God has made women soft, not bony.

But we weren't meant to be plump with fat because we are slaves to food either. That is not a good example for our Lord. We are wearing our sin on our earthly "clothing" for everyone to see.

The Scriptures tell us:

"And take heed to yourselves, lest at any time your hearts be overcharged with surfeiting (overeating, feasting), and drunkenness, and cares of this life, and so that day come upon you unawares." Luke 21:34

****

Discussion:

~Who said that our bodies were the temple of God? (The Bible)

Read: 1 Corinthians 3:16-17

~What happens to a person that defiles the temple of God? (The scriptures say that, "If any man defile the temple of God, him shall God destroy.")
~How important is it that we live according to the "needs" of our bodies rather than our "wants"?
~How can a person defile his "temple"?
~What does it mean to you to eat for health rather than for pleasure?
~Can you give an example?
~Name the foods that would be best for you to eat... (Foods that are created by God, not man.)
~Why is it important to learn about good nutrition as a young lady? (Because a young lady will grow up to be a lady with a husband and children.)
~Why are you not to trust your appetites?
~What is weight control?
~What is gluttony? (Gluttony is the sin of eating unto the lust of the flesh.)

Read: Romans 13:13

~What does it mean "to not make provision for the flesh, to fulfill the lusts thereof"?
~Give some examples of how a person could do this. (Buy ing only junk food to eat, storing up tons of candy in order to sit down and eat it, etc.,)
~Name some foods that you think would be healthy to cook.

Chapter Eight

CLEANLINESS IS NEXT TO GODLINESS (Hygiene)

You may have heard this saying all of your life. But what do you think "cleanliness is next to godliness" means? One meaning might be that it is VERY important to keep yourself clean.

Remember in the last chapter where we were talking about the importance of taking care of our temples, our bodies? And the reason why it is so important to take baths for our health's sake? Well, in this chapter we are going to discuss being clean in other areas. It is sometimes called "hygiene", which simply means to take good care of your outward "dress", or your body.

Wholesomeness

You were created by God to be a girl and to be feminine. Wholesomeness means to be given to sound health or well-being. Basically it means to be a healthy girl or woman! Sound! Both in body and in spirit.

Did you know that the Scriptures promise us a sound mind if we walk in obedience to God's Word? It's true!

"For God has not given us the spirit of fear; but of power, and of love, and of a sound mind." 2 Timothy 1:7

When you are of a sound mind, you will take good care of your temple and be wholesome.

Have you ever been around someone whose whole body is not taken care of? Where their temple is in a state of neglect? It is not a pleasant thing to be around and people will want to avoid them. This is terrible if we are to be a light in this world, an example of those who love God! This is why we must talk about the following delicate subjects.

Bad Breath

If you have ever been around someone with bad breath, or if you have ever had bad breath, you will know that this causes people to immediately back away from you. Imagine telling people about how God is working in your life, and them backing away, wanting to get far away from you, because you have neglected brushing and flossing your teeth!

Always remember to brush your teeth for at least 2 minutes. Another thing to always do is brush in the back of your front bottom teeth by your tongue. This is where a lot of bacteria gather and they are what cause bad breath. Brush your tongue. Flossing is so very important because meat and other articles get stuck in between your teeth and rot. Have you ever opened the refrigerator and smelled meat that has gone bad? This is what is happening in your very mouth.

Brush your teeth three times a day and especially brush and floss before you go to bed at night so food doesn't stay in your mouth while you are sleeping.

This way your teeth will sparkle, your breath will be fresh, and people will want to be near your bright and shining smile!

Body Odor

This is another unpleasant thing to be around. When a person doesn't wash under their underarms properly, a terrible stench arrises. You can usually smell this person from many feet away.

This is because the person has not bathed properly, which means to take a bath every night or every other night, depending on how active you are.

Body odor also becomes a problem if you have not used deodorant.

Be sure to put deodorant on every morning after you have washed your underarms. Some girls, because of how active they are, may need to use it even twice or three times a day.

One caution, though, for your temple's sake... Be aware of deodorants or antiperspirants which have "aluminum alloys" in them. These have been proven to cause terrible diseases.

You might wish to try the salt deodorant sticks which are found in most health food stores, which do not contain these harmful products. They are just salt sticks and kill the bacteria which form under the underarms, which then cause the terrible odor.

Do not use perfume to cover up body odor. This even adds to the problem. If you feel that your deodorant is not working, go to the ladies' room and take a paper towel, or if there is not a paper towel, get some toilet paper, dampen it, and in the privacy of a stall or your own bathroom, clean yourself.

Always, carry a small bottle of talcum powder in your purse. Baby powder is inexpensive and you can buy small bottles of trial size. After you put on deodorant again, use talcum powder on top. It will keep you fresh and your deodorant will work longer!

There is nothing more appealing than a beautiful, wholesome girl who loves God, and smells and looks fresh and clean!

Hair Unkempt

Did you know that God has given woman's hair for her glory and also for a covering?

"But if a woman have long hair, it is a glory to her; for her hair is given her for a covering." 1 Corinthians 11:15

If the Lord views a woman's hair as something important such as this, and if it was worthy of mention in the Holy Scriptures, then shouldn't we learn to also take care of this glory that God has given us?

The Scriptures mention "long hair". The length of "what one thinks is long" should always be determined by your father and then your husband. We shouldn't become contentious regarding others and get out our rulers to measure how long each other's hair is, for that wouldn't be humble in the sight of God.

Let's just assume that the true feminine girl in Christ would obey this and have long hair. So in this portion of the chapter we are going to talk about our long hair and how to care and behave with it.

Have you ever seen a girl twist her hair on the side, or put corners of it into her mouth and suck on it? This wouldn't be proper behavior and would most likely, become a bad habit.

Nor should a girl fix or comb her hair in public.

Hair should always be taken care of in the bathroom, with no one looking on. It is a private matter.

Taking care of long hair is quite easy. The following rules have been used for generations of women and might be something that you could do too:

~Have your hair trimmed every 6 to 8 weeks.

~Brush your hair 50 strokes each morning and evening.

~Find three hair styles that you can do yourself which are tidy and out of your face.

~Shampoo your hair every other day, and switch brands of shampoo once a month in order to stop build up.

~Use a conditioner or detangler in order to stop breakage and split ends.

~After washing your hair, always use a large comb to gently get the tangles out.

~Do not overdry with blow dryers or heating irons.

~Try simple styles that are not ostentatious or calling attention to oneself. This is modesty again.

Dirty and Unpleasant Smelling Clothing

Have you ever worn something for a day or so and then thrown it into your closet or your dresser drawer? If you have ever gone back to that drawer or that closet after a day or two, you will find that there exists a strong odor that is not very pleasant.

If you remember from our previous chapters, this is because our bodies shed cells, and those cells get into our clothing. Even though you may not have spilled food or have gotten dirt on the material, it will still smell from your body.

It is most important that you wash your clothes after two times of wearing them. However, if you only wear this clothing for an hour or two, you do not have to wash them as often. For example, one lovely young lady had a favorite church dress which she only wore for two hours each week. She didn't have to wash that dress for quite some time, and then it had to be dry cleaned.

This brings us to another subject...

Do you help with the laundry?

Have you participated in what it means to keep your clothing clean?

Now is the time to start doing your own laundry. This way you can make sure that you are learning to take care of your clothing that God and your parents have given you.

You are also quite capable of learning how to be tidy in your dress.

Here are the steps for learning to do laundry:

~Take your clothing to your laundry area.

~Separate them into three piles 1) light, 2) dark, and 3) mixed.

~There are 3 different temperatures you should wash each of those colors in. 1) Light should be washed in hot water. 2) Dark is always washed in cold water. 3) Mixed is always washed in medium.

~After you have set the temperature and started the water, add one cap of your laundry detergent.

~In your white or light load, always add 1 cap of your liquid bleach AFTER your water is to the top.

~During your rinse cycle, add softener, such as Downey or some other type.

~Once your load is done, quickly remove it (don't let them sit in the wash machine over night or they will mildew) and place in the dryer.

~Turn your dryer timer on to 45 minutes. After this time is finished, check to see if dry. If not, turn on for another 15 minutes.

~Always fold your clothes immediately, while they are still hot. This cuts down on your ironing.

Keeping Your Face Clean and Blemish Free

Oh, how important it is to keep our faces clean in order to keep blemishes away! This is the last but not least of our subjects for this chapter.

Always remember to wash your face, not once, but twice a day. In the morning when you wake up and at night before you go to bed.

Here is a suggestion for your facial hygiene, in order to keep your face from getting that "grey" color from not being cleansed properly...

~Take a washcloth and take very hot water and first wash your face with that.

~Next take some gentle cleansing liquid, Neutrogena has some very nice soap out there for young ladies, and now gently scrub again with warm water and your washcloth.

~Rinse out the washcloth and then cleanse the face free from all soap. This is very important, for soap can irritate your skin and give blemishes also.

~Then, with your hands (be careful to not make too much of a mess all over the sink) rinse your face with warm water eight times.

~Gently pat your skin dry with a soft, fluffy towel.

~Now, take a cotton ball, and use a skin toner (this helps keep the blemishes away), and go once over all your face and neck.

~Lastly, get a non-oil moisturizer and take some the size of a dime and gently rub it into your skin. Believe it or not, this keeps the oil down after you have washed all excess away.

Now you are ready! Do your hair, get your clean clothes on, and you are prepared to meet your day!

****

Discussion:

Sit down and make a plan for your hygiene.

Here is an example of what your page might look like:

	Face	Hair	Deodorant	Nails	Laundry	Ironing
Monday:						
Tuesday:						
Wednesday:						
Thursday:						
Friday:						
Saturday:						
Sunday:						

Then you check off what you have done. You might wish to add more to this list. The list is important to just help you remember to do these new things!

Read: Psalms 51:2 & 7 "Wash me thoroughly from mine iniquity, and cleanse me from my sin. Purge me with hyssop, and I shall be clean; wash me, and I shall be whiter than snow."

Remember, do not be washed only on the outside, but on the inside too, through Christ!

Chapter Nine

A FEMININE GIRL IN THE FAMILY

Father is the Head of the Home

One of the most wonderful things God has given a young woman is the protection of her father. Our Heavenly Father protects each of us and holds us tenderly in the palm of His hand. God has given as an example, our earthly fathers, who offer their care and protection to their daughters.

There is a hierarchy structure that we have mentioned a little bit in previous chapters. It is called a "patriarchal hierarchy". What does this mean to you as a daughter?

A patriarch is the leader of a family. In the Old Testament Abraham was the leader of his family; Jacob the leader of his twelve sons. In your family, the God-given leader is your father.

"But I would have you know, that the head of every man is Christ; and the head of the woman is the man; and the head of Christ is God." 1 Corinthians 11:3

God has determined that the leadership of a family, and also of the family of God, should be based upon this structure... That God is the head of your father, your father the head of your mother, and the children submitting then under all.

The boss of you and your family then, is your father. God is, of course, the true ruler of everything, but He has delegated the responsiblity of leadership to your dad regarding all family issues.

What does this mean to the young girl?

It means that you must willingly yield yourself to your father's

authority. That is what "submit" means.

For example, there was a young lady who wished to get her ears pieced, and her mother told her that she needed to ask her father. Her father told her that the Scriptures forbade the mutilation of our bodies in any form, and so she quietly agreed with his decision.

This is submitting to the authority of your father.

It is in yielding yourself and all what you do to his will, and by this you will be protected by your father AND your Heavenly Father. Your earthly father will not want any harm to come to you. He will only tell you things that are best for you, even though you may not see the wisdom in them at the time.

Just as our Heavenly Father has given us commandments throughout His Holy Word, in order to protect us from harm, so do our earthly Fathers.

You will live long and have a happy life if you obey your father!

The Correct Way to Ask Permission

Your father wants to give you the best. Remember that when you are asking for things.

There are some things you might remember when you are asking for your father or mother's permission. Some girls might be demanding and also ask in a "spoilt child" type of way. This will not do. It will not do when you are under your father's roof, and it will not do when you are under your husband's roof in the future.

When asking your father for things,

-DO NOT HINT. Your father will probably not understand your hinting; but, also it is not being honest and forthright. Simply ask your father right out.

-DO NOT TRY TO REASON AND GIVE EXCUSES WHEN ASKING. This would be to place yourself above your father and would show a lack of respect. Most of the time, it will make a father or a future husband just say "no" to show that they indeed are in authority, because of you placing yourself above him. It is a way of "coercing" them into doing something, and no one wants to be "coerced".

DO NOT BE DEMANDING when asking your father for anything. To demand anything causes us not to be humble. Remember the scriptures on humility? It is an abomination in the eyes of God for us to demand anything from *anybody*, more or less our own fathers.

When a young girl asks her father for anything, do it simply. Just let your question come as a kind and quiet plea. This shows your father his proper respect and he then will want to do the best thing for you.

Don't ask for things which you know you should not have or that you know he probably will not let you do. If you are asking for something that you already know the answer to is "no", do not ask the question and thereby hurt the good relationship you have with father.

Submitting To Your Father and Trusting His Decisions

What do you do if your father says "no" to something that you feel is unreasonable? Accept it. Do not pout and get angry. Do not show any unkind response. Your father has a perfectly good reason for saying no. If he does not give you a reason, just accept it.

This is where prayer comes in. If you sincerely believe that your father's decision was unreasonable, you must take it to your Heavenly Father. Do not stew in your emotions and build up hatred or anger in any way. You will poison yourself, if you do this! You must pray to your Father in Heaven and tell Him about the situation.

When people do this, miracles happen. Instead of getting angry and ruining your day, you can just sit back in anticipation and watch a miracle happen. But let me caution you, that miracle might be that you understand why your father had the wisdom to tell you no.

Learning From & Confiding in Your Mother

Having a mother is one of the most special gifts that God has given a young girl. Your mother was once young, just like you. She has had to grow up and learn everything that you are learning now.

One of the best presents that God could give a young girl, is the opportunity to become close friends with her mother. In this, you still honor your mother and you still view her with the authority God has given her; but, also you can have her to talk with as a friend. You can confide and tell her your thoughts and hopes and dreams for your future.

Understand that your mother, just like your father, are not perfect. They are human, but if they claim to love God and are trying to follow Him, then you are most fortunate. There are many young girls who are brought up in homes where there are no standards and because of this, it is not a warm and caring home. Thank your Heavenly Father every day that He has given you believing parents.

If they have weaknesses, that is all the more reason why you should be praying for them every single day of your life, in order to help them in the silent realm of prayer.

Try to develop a hobby that you and your mother could do together. It might be knitting, sewing, cooking, or ALL of the above! There are endless opportunities for friendship to be built. Take the time to do it while you have your mother here on earth.

Treatment of Your Sister and your Brother

Most young girls have brothers or sisters to contend with. How do you treat yours? Are you kind to them, or do you talk AT your brothers and sisters, rather than with them?

What does it mean to talk AT someone? Do you know what this means? Have you ever had someone talk AT you rather than with you? Sadly, this is what many siblings do in homes. You can overcome this!

To talk at someone, would be to only give instruction all the time, or only to make comments. You do not expect an answer, you only want to say what you have to say and do not want to listen to them. It is a one way relationship. This is not good.

God would have us listen to others.

"Wherefore, my beloved brethren, let every man be swift to hear, slow to speak, slow to wrath; for the wrath of man worketh not the righteousness of God." James 1:19

Your family are truly the most important people you know. If they have hearts for God, they will not only be your earthly family, but will be your eternal family too!

Remember that you are an example to each of your brothers and sisters. If they misbehave, they can see a shining example how to BE, rather than NOT to be!

Learning to Be Quiet and Gentle
(When Quarrels Happen)

All of us have argued or fought some time in our lives, and I'm sure that you are not an exception. Fighting and strife usually happen when we are wanting our own way. There can't be an argument when one person refuses to argue. It takes two to make an argument.

We must remember that as young girls, we must put aside self-centeredness. You must take responsibility for all the actions that you do. You must not also expect too much from ordinary people like each of your family members. If you don't do these things, you will grow into an adult who will always manipulate and be anxious when things do not go their own way. They will start to blame others for their own mistakes and failures, and they will make unreasonable demands of their own children. This happens if you do not learn how to overcome these things with your own family members now!

If you have brothers, you must help them to understand the

differences between you and them.

Ask your brothers to help you carry things that are too big or heavy for you. Ask you father to explain things to you that you do not know. Have your brothers tell you their favorite foods and try to cook it just like mother!

Sometimes, disagreements might happen between you and your family members. Remember to be gentle in your disagreement. If you cannot be gentle, be quiet. That is the rule of thumb. The following are also some things to remember:

-Do not whine when you are disgruntled.
-Do not yell or ever raise your voice in anger.
-Do not call anyone names.
-Do not be a tale bearer. This means that you do not go to other family members and tell bad things about one to another. This is gossip and poisons a family.
-Do not shriek.
-Do not be quick to cry.

When you are truly angry, walk away and go and pray a bit. This always helps to see things a bit clearer. Ask God, through His precious Son, to help you overcome your weaknesses with your brothers and sisters and your parents.

God will.

He is alive and hears every word you utter. He even knows your very thoughts!

****

Discussion:

~Who is the true head of your home?
~What does "head" mean here? (Leader. Protector.)
~Why should you "submit" yourself to you father and his rules?

(For your own protection.)
~What is the correct way in which to ask permission? (Sim ply, and forthright.)
~What are three things to avoid when asking permission? (Hinting, reasoning/giving excuses, and being demanding.)
~How are you to act when your father says "no"?
~Did you know that God sometimes chastises us?

Read: Hebrews 12:5 (And ye have forgotten the exhortation which speaketh unto you as unto children, My son, despise not thou the chastening of the Lord, nor faint when thou art rebuked of Him, for whom the Lord loveth he chasteneth, and scourgeth every son whom he receiveth. If ye endure chas tening, God dealeth with you as with sons; for what son is he whom the father chasteneth not?)

Read: Proverbs 3:11

Read: Revelation 3:19

~If we are God's, He Himself will chastise us, or correct us. This is what our earthly fathers will also do if they love us. If they do not love us, they will not care enough to do so.

~How should you behave when a quarrel breaks out with your brothers or your sisters?
~Why is prayer so important in a believer's life? (It is our communication with God. Only He can truly help us in all of our life situations. We may think that it is we, ourselves, that do things, but it is all God.)
~When you see good changes in your family members, who has changed them? (It is God who changes the heart.)
~Why then must we never stop praying for our friends and family members? (Because prayer can do things that words can't.)

Chapter Ten

TRUE FEMININITY AND MANNERS

In this chapter we are going to talk about being a "lady" and having manners. Have you ever heard someone say, "My, isn't she such a lady!"? What does this mean to you? What does it mean to be a lady? Do you remember that one meaning of being a lady meant that you are polite and have manners... that you are refined? Refined meaning that you try to behave properly towards others.

There is a difference between manners and etiquette. Manners is having a deep down, heartfelt courtesy towards others. Etiquette is doing things "by the book", or by the etiquette books that society has set for us.

An example of manners would be to kindly see a friend when you are with someone new, and then to introduce the new person around to your friend that is with you and others!

Etiquette is to learn the "proper" way of setting a table. This "proper" way has been established for decades, but the rules for etiquette in America may differ from those, say, in England.

In this chapter, we are going to discuss the art of mannerly etiquette... That of simply being polite and well-bred.

The Polite Girl Starts at Home

Did you know that the best place to learn manners is in your own home? How you treat others is how you will be treated. Remember the golden rule, "Do unto others as you would have them do unto you!"

Good manners will bring peace to a home. They are not like evening clothes, to be brought out only on special occasions. No, they are for everyday life. They are of no value unless they are real, and they cannot be real unless they are based upon kindness and consideration of others. Unless you learn to be kind to the members of your family, you will not be able to be pleasing to those outside of your family.

Start your day out right! Get up when you mother calls you and don't come to the breakfast table in your bathrobe and slippers, with your hair looking as if you had plugged it into a light socket. Think of those who must look at you across the table.

Being punctual to all meals is important. Being late inconveniences others, especially your mother.

Contribute your share of pleasant conversation. Try to have a Bible verse you have been reading about to discuss.

The following deeds are something you may wish to do in your home:

-Respect the property of others.
-Do not be a borrowing pest.
-Return articles promptly and in good condition.
-Curb your curiosity. Mind your own business, and that includes issues of mail, diary's, purses, or other private things.
-Remember the little things. Do your share of the work in your home cheerfully and promptly. Put up magazines, books, and clothes in their proper places.
-Pick up stray hairs from the washbowl. Scrub off the ring in the tub. See that you don't drip puddles on the floor for someone else to step in.
-Be careful to take messages courteously and accurately.
-Don't monopolize the phone.
-If you should drip catsup on your best blouse, get out the clean ing solvent and attend to it yourself.
-Don't invite people over without first asking your parent's per mission.
-Always thank a member of your family for anything that they

have done for you, just as you would strangers.
-Remember that you always let the older members of the family go before you when entering a door. Always pass behind, not in front of people.
-Don't create a disturbance in your home by shouting to some one upstairs or in another room. Go to the place where the person is and speak quietly.
-Help to bring your family even more closely together by always recognizing such special days as birthdays, anniversaries, Mother's Day and Father's Day. Parents and small brothers and sisters love it when their older family members remem ber these special days. It shows love and concern for others. It also teaches the younger children who are watching you, how to treat others.

Good Manners May Be Learned From Others

Who you are around others will always influence how you will grow and behave. It is important to have friends who are also trying to show "good manners" towards others.

Health and cleanliness are also something you may learn from others. This is also a form of good manners. Good posture is a great asset for a young lady. No matter how becoming your clothes may be on your form, the effect is lost if you habitually slouch your shoulders. Try straightening things out. Lift up your head a bit, straighten your back, and pull in your tummy.

Find the friend that is groomed well. What is well-groomed? Well, a well-groomed friend won't have pins where buttons ought to be. They won't have grease spots and perspiration stains on their clothing. They will have their hair tidy.

If you need to improve on your grooming, pay attention to rips in your clothing, making sure to mend those and to restore dangling buttons or snaps to their proper places.

Never go anywhere without a Kleenex or an old-fashioned, dainty, handkerchief.

Be careful that your clothing matches, for example, do not wear sport shoes with an afternoon dress. Do not wear high-heeled shoes with a country-type walking dress.

Avoid extremes in your clothing. This means to not allow yourself to get into the habit of buying "trendy" outfits. These date you and the styles go swiftly out, and you will not be thrifty, as God has called you to be.

Remember the best thing to wear is a smile!

Speaking to Those You Meet

Did you know that the Scriptures are specific in regards to our tongues?

"She openeth her mouth with wisdom; and in her tongue is the law of kindness." Proverbs 31:26

This whole section could be summed up in this proverb. Speak kindly to all those who you meet, and have something worthwhile to say.

If you are terribly shy, try to stop thinking of how you feel and consider putting others around you at ease. Try to make someone feel welcome and comfortable around you. This will give you all you need in order to be around others.

When you meet someone new, always use their name and say, "It's very nice to meet you, Mr. Smith." "It's nice to meet you, Laura." And so on...

When introducing someone, always use their title. This will let the other person know if they are married or not. For example, "Hello, Jane! May I introduce to you Mrs. Harper?" "Mrs. Harper, this is my friend, Miss Jane Randolf."

Always use Mr. and Mrs. when talking to friends of your parents, or those old enough to be your parents. Even though they may not be used to this title, it is a show of respect.

Express Your Appreciation, Always Say, "Thank You!"

A friend was once expressing her sorrow over a family member who never responded to gifts she sent. This dear soul was in her 80's, didn't drive a car, but would walk a long way to a store in order to buy a present for a loved one. When I heard of the effort that was involved in her just purchasing the present and then having to mail it, I just wanted to cry when I heard that the recipient of the gift never even acknowledged getting it!

Always, ALWAYS, remember to send a "thank you" card for any gift or kindness given.

Always remember to say "thank you" for any little consideration given by anyone.

Being Gracious At Table

Graciousness is the name of the game for all of life. Being gracious is to be full of grace, or kind and considerate of all that are around you.

Table manners are very important. We spend three or more hours a day at the table. The following are things to avoid:

-Never do anything to emphasize the fact that you are eating.

-Never lift a dainty little finger when drinking from a cup.

-Never sniff suspiciously at unfamiliar foods.

-Never lick your spoon or fork.

-Never say, "I'm full," "I can't eat again for a week," or other inane vulgarities.

-Never sprawl your legs out far enough under the table to encroach upon the territory of others.

-Never chase a few peas or bread crumbs around your plate as an idle accompaniment to your conversation.

-Never openly estimate the calories being consumed, or compare the vitamin value of string beans and rutabagas.

-Never gulp water. Sip from the glass quietly between bites.

-Never carry off souvenirs from the table.

-Never scoop out a baked potato and churn the contents back and forth with your fork. Eat it from the skin after breaking an opening with your fork.

-Never let your plate look messy.

-Never help yourself too generously, or study a dish before de ciding upon the choicest bit.

-Never observe how others season their food, or how much they eat.

-Never continue after others have stopped eating.

-Never talk or drink with food in your mouth.

-Never find fault with the food.

-Never scratch your head.

-Never load your fork or spoon too heavily.

-Never send your crackers or bread to a watery grave in your soup.

-Never tip back in your chair.

-Never be careless of your personal appearance.

-Never yawn or stretch or be slouchy in your posture at the table.

-Never monopolize the conversation or sit in gloomy silence.

-Never reach across the table or in front of anyone.

-Never take bites too large to control easily.

-Never serve yourself with your own silver.

-Never fuss with your appearance.

-Never cut up all your food before beginning to eat.

-Never put your fingers in your mouth.

-Never appear greedy at any time.

-Never pick your teeth.

-Never eat and run, or stay until your hostess is on the edge of exhaustion.

-Never criticize the table manners of those of another nationality or generation. Customs vary with time and place.

Thing to DO:

-Always return a dinner engagement by a similar invitation.
-Always use your napkin before taking a drink of water.
-Always take your time but try to keep pace with the others eating.
-Always dine rather than eat.
-Always keep hands, arms, and elbows off the table.
-Always be prompt at all meals.
-Always remove your spoon from a cup or tall dish.
-Always sit down and get up from the left side of your chair.
-Always eat from the side of a spoon.
-Always try to eat whatever is served you.
-Always answer definitely when asked to state your preference.
-Always eat leisurely and comfortably, not as if you were anxious about what to do next.
-Always remember that food should be seen, not heard.
-Always practice your good table manners at home.

****

Discussion:

~What is the difference between manners and etiquette?
~Should you have one over the other?

~Check out from your local library a book on table settings and table manners. Read the book and then try to follow its advice when setting your family table.

Read: 1 Corinthians 15:33 (Be not deceived; evil communica tions corrupt good manners.)

~What does this scripture mean to you?

Chapter Eleven

WHAT IS TRUE LOVE?
-"THE TRUE LOVE CHAPTER"-

"Charity suffereth long, and is kind; charity envieth not; charity vaunteth not itself, is not puffed up, doth not behave itself unseemly, seeketh not her own, is not easily provoked, thinketh no evil; rejoiceth not in iniquity, but rejoiceth in the truth; beareth all things, believeth all things, hopeth all things, endureth all things." 1 Corinthians 13:4-7

There are many people who believe in "true love" in a romantic sense. This type of carnal love is to fulfill self and only lasts as long as the "feelings" last.

Many of the fairy tales of our time are based upon this belief. Cinderella, Sleeping Beauty, and most of Grimm's Fairy Tales, had this sensuous philosophy. This is where many people become confused in their life. Always searching for something that is nothing but a "fairy tale" type of love. It is vain. But there is the real "true love". Something so very different from what the world tells us love is.

In this chapter, we are going to talk about the real meaning of "true love". Love that is true. Love that lasts beyond a person's looks or the feelings another makes one feel... This true love is explained completely for us to understand in 1 Corinthians.

"Long Suffering or Patience..."

"Charity suffereth long..."

First, we need to explain what the word "charity" is here in this scripture. It means "love", "true love" for others.

Did you ever think that loving someone meant that we must suffer? Actually, what longsuffering means is to patiently endure wrongs or difficulties. And not just any wrongs or difficulties, but those that come from working with others.

An example would be that instead of crossing others off of our friendship lists because they become burdensome, we learn to bear their burdens. We allow them to inconvenience us with patience, kindness and love. This is what we as believers are called to do.

"The Lord is not slack concerning his promise, as some men count slackness; but is longsuffering to usward, not willing that any should perish, but that all should come to repentance." 2 Peter 3:9-15

Think of your very own sins. Think of how our Heavenly Father patiently endures us. He is longsuffering towards us, and we must learn to be longsuffering towards others who are also growing in Him.

"I therefore, the prisoner of the Lord, beseech you that ye walk worthy of the vocation wherewith ye are called, with all lowliness and meekness, with longsuffering, forbearing one another in love; endeavouring to keep the unity of the Spirit in the bond of peace." Ephesians 4:1-3

As a feminine creature of God, how much more are we to be longsuffering towards all whom God has placed around us. We are not to be quick to anger towards others. If we feel somehow that others may not be as open to God and His ways, we must continue in love towards them with prayer and kindness. This doesn't mean that we are to be "best friends" or close companions with those who may not be walking in a pleasing manner to God, but it does mean that we are to continue hoping and praying and being an example of one who loves God.

And remember this Scripture: *"But the fruit of the Spirit is love, joy, peace, longsuffering, gentleness, goodness, faith, meekness, temperance; against such there is no law."* Galatians 5:22

"Kindness..."

It is easy to be kind to others when they are kind to you. But God has called us to a much more difficult task than that. We are called to be kind to our enemies. We are even to "love" our enemies!

If you think of someone who is kind, what do you picture in your mind? Probably someone who isn't pretending to be kind because she wants someone to view her as a "nice person", but rather you think of someone who is inherently "warmhearted". They would think of being kind no matter what and be truly hurt by those being mean to someone else. That is what you must ask God to have you be.

Did you know that "kind" means to be very friendly, generous, hospitable, warmhearted, good. The next definition is important... It means charitable! Having love. It means helpful, showing sympathy or understanding for others.

If you find that you fall short of all these attributes, ask God to help you develop them in your heart. He is the one who changes us. We cannot change ourselves by simply an act of will. He must change the inside of us. And He will!!!

"But in all things approving ourselves as the minister of God, in much patience, in afflictions, in necessities, in distresses, in stripes, in imprisonments, in tumults, in labors, in watchings, in fastings; by pureness, by knowledge, ***by longsuffering, by kindness****, by*

the Holy Ghost, by love unfeigned!..." 2 Corinthians 6:6

Here it tells us these things are possible by the Holy Spirit!

"Not Being Envious of Others..."

The Scriptures are very clear about "envy". Have you ever felt envious towards someone? This means that you became discontent and resentful when you saw another person's belongings or another's qualities that were different from your own. Envy is when you want something that belongs to someone else.

This could be anything. You might want their home, or you might want their possessions, or their room, or even want to belong in their family rather than your own! Some girls might be more talented than you are and one might even envy their talent and say in their heart, "I wish that I could play the _____ the way they do."

I'm sure that you didn't feel very well at all when you felt this way towards another person. In fact, did you know that you were poisoning yourself and others? Envy is a terrible thing for God's feminine creature to have for anyone else.

"But if ye have bitter envying and strife in your hearts, glory not, and lie not against the truth. This wisdom descendeth not from above, but is earthly, sensual, devilish. For where envying and strife is, there is confusion and every evil work." James 3:14-16

This scripture says it all, for when there is envy, there is strife. But we who love God will give ourselves up to God and try to do things His way, not our own way. We will depart from envy and rather than hating others and envying them, we will love them!!!

"Vaunting not Self; Is not Puffed Up..."

Vaunting is an old word. In the Strong's Concordance, it means to boast or to be a braggart. One dictionary definition says that it means a boastful remark or speech of extravagant self-praise.

Have you ever listened to anyone who is a braggart? I hope you have not; but, if you have, then you know that a braggart continually talks about themselves. This person will let you know everything wonderful they are doing and will pat themselves on the back verbally when talking.

Do not do this. If you ever have an opportunity to boast about your deeds, quickly be very quiet! Close your mouth tightly! Dig your fingernails into your palms, if you must, but do not boast of your own deeds.

"And even as they did not like to retain God in their knowledge, God gave them over to a reprobate mind, to do those things which are not convenient; being filled with all unrighteousness, fornication, wickedness, covetousness, maliciousness; ***full of envy****, murder, debate, deceit, malignity; whisperers, backbiters, haters of God, despiteful, proud,* ***boasters****, inventors of evil things, disobedient to parents..." Romans 1:30*

The opposite of boasting is humility. Remember our lesson on humility? God has called the humble. He detests the proud. To boast about anything you have done makes us detesting in the sight of God.

"This know also, that in the last days perilous times shall come. For men shall be lovers of their own selves, covetous, ***boasters****, proud, blasphemers, disobedient to parents, unthankful, unholy,..." 2 Timothy 3:2*

Did you notice that with boasting also comes the sin of being disobedient to parents? Why do you think this is so? Could it be because being a boaster might make them unteachable and thinking that they know more than their own parents? But the young girl in Christ will put this aside. She will walk according to the teachings of God's Word!!!

"Not Being Unseemly..."

Have you ever heard anyone say, "She certainly behaves unseemly?" Probably not in our generation or in our day. This is an old word that means indecency, shame, inelegant, uncomely. It is to behave yourself in an inappropriate way. In other words, it is to behave in a way that will bring reproach upon the name of our Lord Jesus Christ.

Remember in previous chapters where we have talked about modesty and chastity, and all the other virtues? This is the same thing. It means that you will bring your actions under the control of God's Spirit and do HIS will, not your own.

As a young lady of Christ, you must hold very high the acts of decency, virtue, being comely or beautiful on the inside, and being "elegant", not inelegant.

Isn't that a lovely word... "elegant"? To be elegant means to behave with refinement and grace in your movements, appearance and manners.

People in our day might say that a room is "elegant", but they do not know much about the descriptive word in regards towards a young lady!

But you, my dear, sweet sister, are to be elegant in your deeds, your words, and your movements. Never bringing a bad name to Christ. Always doing the "right" thing, meaning to do what would be pleasing to God through Christ.

"Being Unselfish..."

Selfishness is when a person is concerned chiefly or only with oneself, without regard for the well being of others. It means egotistic, self-centered.

The opposite of being selfish is "LOVING OTHERS", having the best interest in other people above yourself. Did you know our Heavenly Father sent His very own Son, to die for all of us? Because He loved the world so much, He gave His own Son!!!! That is true selflessness. God LOVED us.

If you struggle with being selfish, you might ask God to help you truly love others. This is the only way in which you can die to self. It is through dying to self and living in Christ!

All people are selfish at one time or another. Those who do not love God only live for themselves. We who know Christ, know that we are supposed to live for God. They are at opposite ends.

"But chiefly them that walk after the flesh in the lust of uncleanness, and despise government. Presumptuous are they, ***selfwilled****, they are not afraid to speak evil of dignities..." 2 Peter 2:10*

"Never Thinking Evil of Others..."

Have you ever been around someone who dislikes others, simply because they are "mean-spirited"? This type of person never has anything kind to say about anyone, but will find something bad about everyone and dwell on the bad.

We all have faults. None of us are perfect. A true kindhearted young lady will see these faults, but be "longsuffering and patient" towards others and hope for the best. She will only concentrate on the good that she sees and look for the good first and block out the bad.

There is an old saying, "There is so much bad in the best of us, and so much good in the worst of us, that it hardly behooves any of us, to talk about the rest of us!"

We must think of GOOD things.

"Finally, brethren, whatsoever things are true, whatsoever things

are honest, whatsoever things are just, whatsoever things are pure, whatsoever things are lovely, whatsoever things are of good report; if there be any virtue, and if there be any praise, think on these things." Philippians 4:8

When we come across someone who is behaving themselves unkindly, it might be easy to think evil of them when they are called to mind. How much better if we think instead upon one good thing about that person. Replace evil with good.

Remember, you have faults, and how would you feel if everyone only remembered your faults rather than your good points?

Think on these good things.... !!

"Never Rejoices in Iniquity..."

It might be easy to think of being happy when someone "gets what they deserve". But this is a thought of the world, not a thought of a believer in Christ.

Many of the movies in our time, make a big ending of the bad guy getting his just deserves. If we saturate our minds with these wrong philosophies, we will end up just like the world.

Some day you will most likely be a mother. Do you want your children to get what they deserve when they sin? Our Heavenly Father should only give each of us DEATH. That is what we deserve. That is where His love overcame everything by sending His Son to die for us.

We must remember to never rejoice in any way in sin.

Another thing that women have trouble with is in giving advice and then when the person doesn't take their advice say, "Well, *I told you so."*

This is another way of rejoicing in iniquity. It is rejoicing that something bad happened because they didn't do what you had said to do. It is wrong.

"Discretion shall preserve thee, understanding shall keep thee... from those who.... rejoice to do evil, and delight in the frowardness of the wicked." Proverbs 2:14

"Rejoiceth not when thine enemy falleth, and let not thine heart be glad when he stumbleth, lest the Lord see it, and it displease Him, and He turn away His wrath from him." Proverbs 24:17

"Rejoicing in Truth..."

The Scriptures command us to always rejoice in truth. What is the truth? According to the Word of God, Truth is what is fact, actuality, according to God's Word. It also means sincerity, integrity; honesty. In other words, we are to rejoice in the Scriptures, we are to rejoice continuously, even in trials.

One way to look at it, is to have a heart of happiness because you are sincerely trying to do what God says to do. It is rejoicing in this very life that God has given you. He has given believers a purpose for living, a goal in life, and that goal is HEAVEN through God's Son, Jesus Christ.

Imagine life without God. This is the state in which the world lives. They have no purpose, they have no plan or goal. But we as believers have a wonderful goal! It is to live out God's will through His Holy Word.

"For the hope which is laid up for you in heaven, whereof ye heard before in the Word of the Truth of the gospel; which is come unto you, as it is in all the world; and bringeth forth fruit, as it doth also in you, since the day ye heard of it, and knew the grace of God in Truth!".... Colossians 1:5-6

Because we have this hope we are to be diligently studying God's Truth, His Word! Anyone who claims to love God will love His instruction book, the Bible. The Bible tells us how to live our lives and gives us all we need to know on this earth.

"Study to shew thyself approved unto God, a workman that needeth not to be ashamed, rightly dividing the Word of Truth." 2 Timothy 2:15

"Bearing all Things, Believing all Things, Enduring all Things..."

We are called to bear all things, believe all things, endure all things. When we have a heart that loves others, this is something that would come easy.

Think of someone that you love very much. Have they ever done you a wrong? Have they ever been unkind to you? Probably so. Does that stop you from loving them? No. It doesn't. It may hurt you a bit to be treated unkindly, but you will forgive them and you don't stop loving them.

This is what the Bible is telling us to do. We must bear wrongs done to us.

The world will say, "How can you put up with this person treating you so..." But as a Christian, we are to put up with unfairness and more.

How can we continue doing so? Because we have HOPE. We have hope that these people will grow into the knowledge of Christ and His Word. We can never give up on this hope.

"Hatred stirs up strife, but love covereth all sins." Proverbs 10:12

When you love someone, you will forgive and forbear with one another. You don't hold grudges. You forget, just as we hope that God will forgive and forget our sins.

This is true love...

****

Discussion:

~What is meant by long suffering?
~Give an example of how you are to be patient and long suffering towards others...
~Describe how you are to be kind.
~What is the difference of "seeming" to be kind, and truly "being" kind?
~What in the danger of envy?
~What other negative trait goes along with envy? (Strife)
~What is strife?
~What does the word "VAUNT" mean?
~Describe what a braggart is. Give an example of bragging.
~What do the scriptures say regarding a "boaster"?
~What goes along with boasting? (Being disobedient to par ents.)
~Why do you think they go hand in hand?
~What does it mean to be "unseemly".
~How can you behave "elegantly"?
~Describe a selfish person.
~Describe an unselfish person.
~What is the answer to ending unselfishness? (Truly loving others.)
~What is a "mean-spirited" person? What are their tenden cies?
~What are we to think upon as believers? (Things that are true, honest, just, pure, lovely, of good report, virtue, and those things of praise.)
~What does it mean to "rejoice in iniquity".
~Give some examples.
~Describe "rejoicing in truth".
~What does "hope" have to do with rejoicing in truth? (We rejoice constantly because of the hope we have within us.)
~Describe the difference between true love and the world's carnal love.

Chapter Twelve

THE NEED FOR CHRIST IN OUR LIVES

Many people try to be "good". They try to do the "right" thing. In our world today, though, people make up on their own what they think is "good" or "bad". Those who don't know God through His Son, Jesus, might look at what they are doing as being "good and right", but according to God's Word, what they are doing is *wrong*.

The Scriptures tell us *"All the ways of a man are clean in his own eyes; but the Lord weigheth the spirits." Proverbs 16:2*

In our own eyes we may seem to be doing the "right" thing. The public education system believes that the right thing to do is to teach that there is no difference between being a girl or a boy. They teach that it is wrong to teach a young girl to be a mother at home and to have home duties. They believe that the "right" way is to have women competing with men in providing for their households. They even go so far as to say that if a woman does not work, that she is not "doing her part in helping the husband".

But this is deception. This is not what the Scriptures tell us to do. But you can argue with a person very strongly about these things, and if the Bible doesn't mean anything to them, you are wasting your time.

A person who knows Christ, will have the Scriptures as the guidebook for living. A person who does not know Christ, can only live by their own "feelings". They live from emotion to emotion, not by any "rule" book that would give them guidelines to a healthy, long and full life.

A person that does not have a love for God and His ways will view those that do love God as foolish.

"For the preaching of the cross is to them that perish foolishness; but unto us which are saved it is the power of God. For it is written, I will destroy the wisdom of the wise, and will bring to nothing the understanding of the prudent. Where is the wise? Where is the scribe? Where is the disputer of this world? Hath not God made the foolish the wisdom of this world? For after that in the wisdom of God the world by wisdom knew not God, it pleased God by the foolishness of preaching to save them that believe." 1 Corinthians 1:18+

"Because the foolishness of God is wiser than men; and the weakness of God is stronger than men. For ye see your calling, brethren, how that not many wise men after the flesh, not many mighty, not many noble, are called; but God hath chosen the foolish things of the world to confound the wise; and God hath chosen the weak things of the world to confound the things which are mighty; and base things of the world, and things which are despised, hath God chosen, yea, and things which are not, to bring to nought things that are. That no flesh should glory in His presence." 1 Corinthians 1:25+

The importance of living a life with Christ cannot be stressed enough. Living a life without Him leaves a person feeling empty, with no purpose, and will cause them to be totally self-centered and self-absorbed. They might seem to be a "loving" person, but how can anyone know "true love" unless they know Christ? They can't.

You may have *known about* God and His Son through the Holy Spirit all your life. But knowing about someone and *truly knowing them* are two different things.

Do you really know God? Or do you simply know about Him? If

you have any doubt about this at all, please stop right here and truly seek God in prayer through His Son, Jesus Christ. Talk to your parents about it and ask them to help you *know* God.

It isn't a magic formula, you know. It is simply knowing that you believe in His Son, that He died on the Cross in your place, for your sins, and that He then rose from death and conquered death in victory! You know that He did this for you so that you could now have access to the Father through Him. You see, God couldn't look upon us because of our sin, but when He sent Jesus to die for us, Jesus who was without sin, He took upon Himself those sins, and now we have pure access to the Father. We can now go straight to God through His wonderful Son.

When you believe this and you have this knowing in your heart, you will want to do what God tells you to do. When you sin, your heart will be grieved. You will not want to do things that aren't pleasing to your Heavenly Father.

You will also want to know more about God and His ways. You will need to have your mind renewed from your "old ways". This comes through the reading of His Word, the Bible.

And it's not just reading the Scriptures. There are many people that "know" God's Word. Even Satan knows God's Word. But more importantly, you must be a DOER of God's Word.

That's what this chapter is all about. It is about the importance of knowing God and being around those that are like-minded in this knowing and loving Him.

The Need for Godly Fellowship

When you are a Christian, you might have to be around people who do not know God. You might have to be in situations where people are "saying" they know God, but their actions are quite different from what the Bible says to do. In any of these situations, you probably aren't truly having "Godly fellowship".

What is "Godly fellowship?

In order to be able to be strong in Christ, we must be around people who are also trying to follow God and His ways. When we are only around people who do not know God, we might tend to get persuaded that their way, the way the world lives without the instruction of God's Word, is right!

The Scriptures tell us that it is not good for us to befriend those that do not love God.

"Else if ye do in any wise go back, and cleave unto the remnant of these nations, even these that remain among you, and shall make marriages with them, and go in unto them, and they to you, know for a certainty that the Lord your God will no more drive out any of these nations from before you; but they shall be snares and traps unto you, and scourges in your sides, and thorns in your eyes, until ye perish from off this good land which the Lord your God hath given you." Joshua 23:12-13

"Be ye not unequally yoked together with unbelievers; for what fellowship hath righteousness with unrighteousness? And what communion hath light with darkness? And what concord hath Christ with Belial? Or what part hath he that believeth with an infidel? Wherefore come out from among them, and be ye separate saith the Lord, and touch not the unclean thing." 2 Corinthians 6:14

Why are we not to befriend the world? Because it truly can become a snare to us.

When we see that other people are doing things, say EVERYBODY is doing something that is not pleasing to God, something inside us might say, "Well, look, this person whom I admire is doing this, so... it must not be so BAD if *they* are doing it now, is it?"

Because of our associations with people who are not following God, our convictions might not stand. We might become double minded in all of our ways.

But! If we have fellowship with others we are made strong...

"He that walketh with wise men shall be wise; but a companion of fools shall be destroyed." Proverbs 13:20

"Behold, how good and how pleasant it is for brethren to dwell together in unity! It is like the precious ointment upon the head, that ran down upon the beard, even Aaron's beard; that went down to the skirts of his garments. As the dew of Hermon, and as the dew that descended upon the mountains of Zion; for there the Lord commanded the blessing, even life for evermore!" Psalms 133:1-3

It is very difficult sometimes to walk as God says to do, contrary to what the world says to do. That is why we must have others who believe as we do around us.

"Comfort yourselves together, and edify one another, even as also ye do. We exhort you, brethren, warn them that are unruly, comfort the feebleminded, support the weak, be patient toward all men." 1 Thessalonians 5:11 & 14

When you choose your friends, choose to be with those that love God and will support you and others in your walk with God. Do not make friends with the world.

"Ye adulterers and adulteresses, know ye not that the friendship of the world is enmity with God? Whosoever therefore will be a friend of the world is the enemy of God." James 4:4

Relationship With God

As a young woman, the number one most important thing is to have a relationship with God. Some people believe that it is important to have relationships with other girls. This is something to really stop and ponder on.

Many young ladies, unknowingly will substitute earthly, carnal relationships for a true relationship with God. But God is very faithful. He wants ALL of us. He is a JEALOUS God. He wants to be our very best friend. He is our BRIDEGROOM.

"For thou shalt worship no other god; for the Lord, whose name is Jealous, is a jealous God." Exodus 34:14

"God is jealous, and the Lord revengeth..." Nahum 1:2

God is jealous of anything other than HIM being first in our lives. He wants us to love Him with ALL our heart, ALL our souls, and ALL our minds. Not just a little section of our life on Sundays portioned out to Him.

This is why HE is to be our very best friend. When you have troubles in life, do you go to your earthly friend and tell your troubles to them? Or do you first go to your Heavenly Father? When you are sad and lonely, do you seek out an earthly companion? Or do you go fall on your knees before God and seek Him to be your Comforter?

Remember that He has not left us alone on earth. He gave the Comforter to be with us until the end of the earth.

"I will pray the Father, and he shall give you another comforter, that he may abide with you forever. Even the Spirit of truth; whom the world cannot receive, because it seeth him not, neither knoweth him; but ye know him; for he dwelleth with you, and shall be in you." John 14:16 &17

"But the Comforter which is the Holy Ghost, whom the Father will send in my name, He shall teach you all things, and bring all things to your remembrance, whatsover I have said unto you." John 14:26

Many people seek comfort from other people, this is fine, AFTER you have first sought comfort from God.

If you are going to have a home and a family, and if you are going to be obedient to the Scriptures which tell young women to be "keepers at home", you might find that you feel a bit lonely at times during the day. This is normal. This is because you are not out there in the work force surrounded by hundreds of other working women. You are *quietly* at home.

If you find that even now, as you are at home, that you are feeling lonely, this might be because you are not spending enough joyous time in the Word of God, reading about Him and His ways. You may have not been *renewing* your minds as we are taught. Therefore, you start getting carnal and selfish in your thoughts and are only thinking of how "you" feel, rather than concerning yourself with those who are around you.

Remember, when you are walking in God and His ways, all thoughts of selfish motives will fall off of you and you will be happy and content because you have relationship with Him! And in that is true joy and happiness!!!!

Talk to God in Prayer Continuously

Prayer, according to the Strong's Concordance, simply means to "talk to God". It doesn't mean that you are to "memorize" a specific prayer and say it over and over. That is called a "mantra" and is not of the Christian belief. God's Word tells us not to do this type of praying.

"But when you pray, use not vain repetitions, as the heathen do, for they think that they shall be heard for their much speaking. Be not ye therefore like unto them; for your Father knoweth what things ye have need of before ye ask Him." Matthew 6:7

When we pray, Jesus told us to go to God as a Father. He said to say, "Heavenly Father, or our Father which is in Heaven". We are to go to God as a child goes to his parents. Remember, this is how you talk to God. He hears you. He knows you. He created you. You are His very own child and He loves you very, very dearly.

Do not think that He doesn't care about little things in your life. If God cares enough to number the very hairs on your head, he must care about every little thing in your life!

"Are not two sparrows sold for a farthing? And one of them shall not fall on the ground without your Father. But the very hairs of your head are all numbered. Fear ye not therefore, ye are of more value than many sparrows." Matthew 10:30

Having Virtue by Boldly Standing for Christ and His Teachings

When you know God and are living to please Him, you will come to the point where you no longer care what men think about you, but will only care what God thinks.

If you live your life worrying about what other people think about what you do, then you are what is called a "menpleaser".

"...Not with eyeservice, as menpleasers; but as the servants of Christ, doing the will of God from the heart. With good will doing service, as to the Lord, and not to men; knowing that whatsoever good thing any man doeth, the same shall he receive of the Lord, whether he be bond or free." Ephesians 6:6

We are to be courageous as believers, willing to do what God has called us to do. Never to fear men, but to fear God.

"Fear not them which kill the body, but are not able to kill the soul; but rather fear Him which is able to destroy both soul and

body in hell." Matthew 10:28

"We must all appear before the judgment seat of Christ; that every one may receive the things done in his body, according to that he has done, whether it be good or bad. Knowing therefore the terror of the Lord, we persuade men." 2 Corinthians 5:10-11

This is how we are to live for God. We know that we will give an account for every thing we have done and every word we have uttered during this short life on earth. Therefore, why will we ever worry about what men think of us? We, as true believers in God through Christ, will only worry about what God thinks!

****

Discussion:

~What are some things that may seem "right to man" but are not "right in the eyes of God?
~What is the difference between living by "feelings" and liv ing by the "truth of God's Word".
~Describe the difference of "knowing about God" and "know ing God"....
~Why is it important that we have "Godly Fellowship"?
~What happens if the only friends around us are those that do not know or follow God's Word?
~What does the Bible say God is regarding fellowship? (It says that God is a JEALOUS God.)
~What does it mean by this?
~Will God ever leave us? What did He send to us? (The Comforter.)
~What is prayer? (It simply means to communicate or to talk with God.)
~What is a menpleaser?
~Who are we to please?

Chapter Thirteen

THE CAPABLE GIRL

In an earlier chapter we mentioned that a young lady is to be capable but not independent. We are going to go into being "capable" a bit more throughout this next lesson. Being capable is something that people hope that they might be, but not much is taught about it any more.

The word "CAPABLE" means that you are very competent and efficient; that you are able to perform duties. It also means that you are qualified for service!

As a young woman, you are being trained to become a future mother of tomorrow. Your duty is very, very grave and important, for you will be training the generations of people of tomorrow. The awesome responsibility of this could be overwhelming, but it won't be with the power of God's Spirit upon you! You will be able to be quite capable of training your children. The thing you must remember, is that there is a reason you are in training right now! And that you can do all things through Christ Jesus who strengthens you.

Try to remember that all you are learning now is to help you for your future as a wife and mother. When life seems to become monotonous and you become discouraged, remember how important you are to your Heavenly Father. He has placed a great responsibility in your hands and He trusts you to carry it out. It is that of future motherhood.

What a wonderful honor and blessing this position is. And it is up to you to be willing to follow God and His ways and learn everything you can to be pleasing to Him in this function of womanhood.

This is what it is to be capable. You are going to learn to become a capable woman as you grow as a capable young girl.

Bright and Cheerful, and Up Early in the Morning!

There is an old saying that goes, "Early to bed, early to rise, makes a man healthy, wealthy and wise." There is another that follows, "Late to bed, up all night; means pain in the head; and quick to fight."

There are many people who might discourage you from trying to go to bed early and waking up early. It is because many of these people tend to stay up entertaining themselves one way or another, as is the way of the world. They find it difficult to go to sleep and then even more difficult to get up early and start the day before the sun rises.

What does the Bible have to say about this? The Scriptures give us an example of Godly womanhood in the book of Proverbs.

"She riseth also while it is yet night, and giveth meat to her household, and a portion to her maidens." Proverbs 31:15

This is telling us that the virtuous woman arises before the sun gets up. If you ever have had roosters, you know that the roosters crow at dawn, when it is still dark outside and just before the sun gets up over the horizon.

Why would this be important? Have you ever thought to truly dissect the reason it benefits the mother of the house to get up before everyone else? When you have many little ones, it is very difficult to get some things done when they are under foot. Arising before the children, first, allows time alone with God; next, will allow some time for prayer with your husband (when you have one); then, you will be able to organize your day quietly, putting in order all that must be done.

Even now, dear sister, is the time for you to start this important habit. Prioritize your day. Make a list of things which you must do for each day of your life. Put the most important things that you must do at the top and then write the things you would like to accomplish underneath those.

If you can get into the habit of prioritizing your life, you will become an organized woman when you are older!

Go to Bed at a Certain Time

Try to get in the habit of going to bed at a certain time.

Did you know that scientists have just discovered that the best medicine for those who are insomniacs (people who can't sleep at night) is for them to go to bed at a certain time every evening? They found that if they did not vary in their bedtime, that they would automatically start falling asleep at that time every night and would have a peaceful sleep!

How much more should we as Christians be organized even in our bedtimes?

Someday, you will have children whom you will be responsible for. It is very important that you give your children a consistent home life. By giving them a bedtime, you are giving them a solid environment for healthy living. When you allow your children to just "live unto themselves and decide for themselves when they are tired", it shows that you do not care about them. Children need structure. The body works best when it is on a schedule. Chaos causes stress, which has been proven to cut your life short.

Many people use the evening for carnal entertainment. The scriptures tell us that we are not to behave as does the world and fill our lives with fleshly entertainments. We are told to live soberly and that we are not children of the night.

"Ye are all the children of light, and the children of the day; we are not of the night, nor of darkness." Thessalonians 5:5

Did you know that eventually we will not need to sleep? At least we know that there will be no night in the new heaven and the new earth. Isn't that interesting? Perhaps it is because we will have bodies that won't need to rest or rejuvenating any more.

"And I saw no temple therein; for the Lord God Almighty and the Lamb are the temple of it. And the city had no need of the sun, neither of the moon, to shine in it; for the glory of God did lighten it, and the Lamb is the light thereof.... And the gates of it shall not be shut at all by day; ***for there shall be no night there!****" Revelation 21:25*

We await with great joy this day of our Lord!

Always Be "ON TIME"

Another part of being "capable" is to be kind to others in regards to their time. Most of us only have so many hours given to us by our Heavenly Father. How unkind and unthoughtful it is for us to be late and to keep others waiting for us.

The world will sometimes give the excuse that it is "in style" to be a little bit late... To make one's "appearance". Did you know that there is no such thing as being "fashionably late"? There is only such a thing as being unfashionably rude...!

There was once a young girl who would tell her friends that she would be at a cooking class at a certain time. She would always be 30 minutes or more late. She would run in, miss most of the cooking course, and then ask questions about what she missed. This was most unkind towards all the people who had taken the time to be there when they were supposed to be.

Eventually, she was no longer invited to the cooking classes, or to any other event, you might guess!

Keeping Your Word

What does it mean, "to keep your word"? Keeping your word

means that you will always do what you say you will do. It means that you mean exactly what you say.

The world may tell us, "that it is a woman's prerogative to change her mind". This is so very wrong. When a person "changes her mind", this is a nice way of saying that you can't count on, or trust a thing they say.

As one who is representing Christ here on earth, it is so important that you can be trusted to mean what you say.

Did you know that you will be asked by God to account for every idle word you have uttered in your life?

"But I say unto you, that every idle word that men shall speak, they shall give account thereof in the day of judgment. For by thy words thou shalt be justified, and by thy words thou shalt be condemned". Matthew 12:36-37

"But above all things, my brethren, swear not, neither by heaven, neither by the earth, neither by any other oath; but let your yea be yea; and your nay, nay; lest ye fall into condemnation." James 5:12

What does the scripture say happens if your yeas aren't yeas? Well, it says that you will fall into condemnation. Don't you think that if you are claiming to be Christ's and you are constantly walking in a manner that brings Him to shame that you couldn't help but to fall into condemnation?

The Scriptures do not lie. If we do not walk uprightly and honest in all things and in all our dealings with others, we become a reproach to the Word of God. So, live simply and honestly, being someone whom others may count on.

Controlling Your Temper

Have you ever been angry about something and lost your temper over it? Actually, if you have "lost your temper", where did you lose it? Sometimes, if we took this literally, it would be quite nice if we could "lose our tempers" permanently!

There is nothing that causes a young girl to become more ugly in her appearance than when she gives herself over to anger.

The Scriptures tell us that we are to be SLOW to wrath, or anger:

"Wherefore, my beloved brethren, let every man be swift to hear, slow to speak, slow to wrath." James 1:19

Did you know that we are not to be friends with people that are angry? It's true...

"Make no friendship with an angry man, and with a furious man thou shalt not go; lest thou learn his ways, and get a snare to thy soul." Proverbs 22:24-25

The reason we are to stay away from angry people is that anger is catching. For example, you can have a friend who is angry over something someone did to them. They can then tell you all the awful things that this person did, and soon, YOU will find yourself angry over something that isn't even related to you. You have *caught* their anger!

"Be ye angry, and sin not. Let not the sun go down upon your wrath. Let all bitterness, and wrath, and anger, and clamor, and evil speaking , be put away from you, with all malice." Ephesians 4:26 & 31

"But now ye also put off all these, anger, wrath, malice..." Colossians 3:8

What goes with anger? Well, here the Scriptures tell us anger comes with wrath and malice. The opposite of these things is love! We, as God's feminine creation, are to walk in love, which stops anger! wrath! and malice!

God would have us love one another rather than to be angry all the time. This is HIS way, and we are to live for Him rather than for our "feelings".

****

Discussion:

~What is a "CAPABLE GIRL"?
~What are you to become capable of? (Of being a mother, wife and a feminine creature God has created for His service.)
~Why is it important to get up early?
~What happens if you get up late? (You literally LOSE hours of your life through sleeping. You give your life away.)

Read: Proverbs 24:30 "Yet a little sleep, a little slumber, a little folding of the hands to sleep; so shall thy poverty come as one that travelleth; and thy want as an armed man."

~Why should you learn to have a regular bedtime?
~What does "being late" show others? (It shows that you are selfish and inconsiderate of others.)
~What do "keeping your word" and "being on time" have in common? (When you say you'll be someplace at a certain time, you will keep your word to be there!)
~What does God think about "angry people"?
~Why are we not to befriend them?
Rather than "being angry", what should we be towards others?

Chapter Fourteen

FRIENDSHIPS

"A man that hath friends must shew himself friendly; and there is a friend that sticketh closer than a brother." Proverbs 18:24

In this life here on earth there is no better gift than having a true friend that loves God the same as you do. Having a friend is being a friend, just as the Scripture above tells us.

As a young girl, you will have friends who are both male and female. There is something that you need to think about... The world may be coarse and tease little boys and girls about being sweethearts simply because they are friends. This is very wrong and shows an evil heart. Do not ever listen nor follow along with this type of talking.

You will have friends that are boys and girls as a young girl, but they are to be relationships that are pure in the sight of God. They are to be noble relationships, a relationship that brings God glory.

The Blessing of Christian Friendship

"Let the word of Christ dwell in you richly in all wisdom; teaching and admonishing one another in psalms and hymns and spiritual songs, singing with grace in your hearts to the Lord." Colossians 3:16

There is a type of relationship which the world calls "friendship". In reality it is nothing more than being an acquaintance. An acquaintance is knowing someone because you see them, but you have never really been able to share what you truly believe. Most likely, if you shared what you truly believe, they probably wouldn't think too highly of you.

On the other hand, a true friend is someone with whom you share your heart with and they too have the same heart with the same interests.

"As in water face answereth to face, so the heart of man to man." Proverbs 27:19

This is how you can tell whether a person is an acquaintance or a friend. In the world in which we live we may find some very nice people who are not believers in the Lord Jesus. They may do nice things and they may be kind to you, but in reality you will not have anything in common. The reason this is, is because they are not following the same King as you are.

You are following God, and His Word means something very important to you. When you believe in our Savior, you are trying to do what He says to do.

How sad it is when you are trying to live your life according to God's ways, and you are around people who don't believe in how you are trying to live.

What happens is that they will become a discouragement rather than an encouragement. Many times young ladies who have once had a heart towards God, have had their hearts turned away from His ways because of a worldly influence in their life.

But on the other hand, if you have true friends around you who hold the Word of God as their instruction book for living, they will encourage you when you are disobeying His ways. They will love you enough to say, "Wait a minute! You are thinking this way, but the Word of God says this..."!

This is what a true friend does. They will hold you up as you will hold them up. You will sharpen them as they sharpen you!

"Iron sharpeneth iron; so a man sharpeneth the countenance of his friend." Proverbs 27:17

When true friends are seeking the Word of God each on their own, when they meet they will have wonderful things to talk about. Not things such as dress, or music groups, or boys, as the worldly society does. No, true friends in Christ will be excited about what they have been studying in the Bible! When they get together they will talk about new recipes, family, and the homes they hope to have some day... the topics are endless!!!!

And what wonderful fellowship it is. This is the type of friendship that pleases God.

"Two are better than one; because they have a good reward for their labor. For if they fall, the one will lift up his fellow; but woe to him that is alone when he falleth, for he hath not another to help him up. Again, if two be together, then they have heat; but how can one be warm alone? And if one prevail against him two shall withstand him, and a threefold cord is not quickly broken." Ecclesiastics 4:9-12

Not Allowing a Peer to Pressure

In the world there is something called "peer pressure". What is this? Well, it means when a young man or woman allows someone else to force them, either with words of persuasion, or with promises of praise or flattery, to do things that are not pleasing to God.

Is there "peer pressure" around you? Well, wherever there are people, there will be someone trying to influence you one way or another. This is what we were talking about regarding the differences between an acquaintance and a true friend.

A true friend wouldn't want you to do things that would be contrary to God's Word. On the other hand, an acquaintance that doesn't follow God and His ways would only have their own self-interest at heart.

Sadly, we all are selfish at times and only want things our way. We might be "pressuring others". Sometimes, even you might try to get your own way, or sway others to do your will.

Even with your parents, have they ever told you "no" to something, and because this was against your will, or against what you wanted, you made excuses or maybe even argued with them, hoping to change their minds? This is a form of "peer pressure".

Sometimes, even our most trusted friend, might be tempted into doing something wrong and having you go along with them. The Scriptures warn us about this...

"My son, if sinners entice thee, consent thou not. If they say, 'Come with us.. Cast in thy lot among us; let us all have one purse...' My son, walk not thou in the way with them; refrain thy foot from their path." Proverbs 1:10-15

A true friend would tell them, "No! Many may go that way, but I cannot!"

"One sinner destroyeth much good." Ecclesiastics 9:18

It only takes one apple to spoil the whole bushel... Make sure that you are not in the same barrel!

Good, Not Bad Friendships

You must be very careful in your choice of friends. One thing to always remember is to not become too intimate. You must learn to be noble enough to keep your own secrets, or have your own secret with your mother.

There have been young girls who had no idea of keeping family affairs to themselves and would tell their friends things that happened in the privacy of their own homes.

There was one little girl who told her friend, "We have only 12 plates to eat on, so when we have company, my mother has to go without or I have to wait."

This kind of talk would have brought mortification to her mother if she would have known that the little girl had told this family business to someone else!

One young lady was listening to her father's conversation when he was talking about selling his car, and when a price was mentioned piped up, "But, Dad, you said that you would take $2,000, not $2,500!" So, by her thoughtless interruption, she made her father look bad.

Too much intimacy with a friend is wrong. There is an old saying...

"Familiarity breeds contempt."

This means that we allow others to be too familiar and that we haven't allowed the special distances that God has set up through His hierarchy. That hierarchy is God is the head of Christ; Christ is the head of your father (and eventually your husband); and then, the husband is the head of the wife (your mother and eventually your husband will be the head over you). By allowing anyone other than this safety net to be over you is allowing danger to enter into your life.

For instance, it is wrong for a friend to become more important to you than your Heavenly Father, or more than your mother and father. There are even some marriages where the wives allow their sisters in Christ, and that relationship, to be more important to them than their relationship with Christ and their own husbands! This is a terrible thing to allow. God would have you to keep your relationships pure in Him, by having your friendships based upon the Word of God. Then your friendships will make you stronger in Christ rather than weaker.

Keeping a Relationship Pure

God tells us in His Word that we are to keep ourselves pure and unspotted from the world.

"Every man that hath this hope in him purifieth himself, even as he is pure." 1 John 3:3

"Cleanse your hands, ye sinners, and purify your hearts, ye doubleminded." James 4:8

These Scriptures talk about the purity of our hearts. It is our hearts that God is concerned with. The following rules regarding friendship might help you:

1. Choose your friends wisely; don't simply *fall* into a friendship with someone.
2. Have your friendship based upon a mutual love of the Word of God. Then your friendship will last throughout eternity.
3. Do not allow too much familiarity. Keep a certain distance from them by keeping your parents, or your husband in the future, between you.
4. Do not ever allow sin to rule in your conversation. Base your conversation on Philippians 4:8.
5. Agree with your friend that you will always base your beliefs upon the Word of God. If you find something that they are saying or doing that does not line up with the Word of God, that you will lovingly show them what the Word says. **That** is true friendship and love.
6. That if a friend falls away from God's Word and walks in rebellion towards God after you have gone to them, and they still refuse to walk in His ways any more after you have tried to reason the Scriptures with them lovingly, then you will separate from them. 1 Corinthians 5:11.

****

Discussion:

~What is the difference between an acquaintance and a friend?
~What should a friendship be based upon? (The mutual love of God and a respect and dedication to the Word of God.)
~What is "peer pressure"?
~Have you ever been under pressure to do something that isn't pleasing to God?
~Have you ever tried to get your own way?
~What does it mean to you to "not become too intimate with friends"?
~Why would this be important? (So that you will always have God first, and not be influenced negatively.)
~Have a you ever had a friend that loved God as much as you do?
~How can you tell that they do?
~Why is it important that your parents and then your husband always be your *best friends*?
~Why must you separate when a friend turns from God? (2 Peter 2:18 says, For when they speak great swelling words of vanity, they allure through the lusts of the flesh, through much wantonness, those that were clean escaped from them who live in error. While they promise them liberty, they them selves are the servants of corruption; for of whom a man is overcome, of the same is he brought in bondage.)
~Would you have anything really in common with a friend who doesn't love God any more?
~Why would the world consider this "harsh treatment"? (Be cause the world has a rule of tolerance, in that we aren't to make any judgements of what is right and wrong any more. They teach that everyone has their own set of rules of what is right and wrong and that we are to respect them. This isn't what believers in God follow. We follow God's set of rules of right and wrong, even though the world will mock and make fun of us as we follow them.)

Chapter Fifteen

LEARNING HOW TO CONVERSE WITH OTHERS

Learning how to talk with other people might not seem to be important right now, but it is one of the most important aspects of being a believer. How you converse with others is how you will be a light unto the world.

Christ told us all to, "Go into all the world and preach the gospel."

As women, we do this through our actions as well as our words.

If you are painfully shy, which there is absolutely nothing wrong with being shy, you might want to pay careful attention regarding the following suggestions to help you in this area.

The Importance of Being Well-Read on Womanhood

The Bible tells us in 1 Corinthians 14:34, "Let your women keep silence in the churches; for it is not permitted unto them to speak; but they are commanded to be under obedience, as also saith the law, and if they will learn any thing, let them ask their husbands at home; for it is a shame for women to speak in the church."

This is a very hard Scripture if you are a woman. In our day, we are taught that women and men are equal in every area. Many women get hurt and very angry when they read this Scripture.

Please know, that one belief that our Grandparent's generation had concerning this passage was that the men were to be the heads of the household. When a woman took the place of the man, the man started becoming submissive to the woman, and the woman started becoming domineering and authoritative. They believed that by having the women keep quiet, and keeping their children quiet, that the men could then take their rightful positions as the head of the household and the spiritual head of the family.

But this doesn't mean that women weren't to talk at all! Oh, no! Women and men were called to encourage one another daily. The older women were taught to teach the younger women homemaking skills. How could they do this if they were silent all the time? They couldn't! We are all called to converse and encourage one another.

This leads to the main thought of this chapter. Every word you speak should be to encourage those who hear you.

Now what would a young lady have to speak about in order to encourage those around her? Wouldn't it be wonderful if you could be an encourager in the Scriptures regarding Christian womanhood?

And in order to encourage others, you must have knowledge of such things. This is where studying what the Bible has to say regarding this fascinating subject comes in. You must be well-versed and knowledgable on Christian femininity.

Do you remember what your older sisters in Christ are to teach you?

The Bible says, *"The aged women likewise, that they be in behavior as becometh holiness, not false accusers, not given to much wine, teachers of good things; that they may teach the young women to be sober, to love their husbands, to love their children, to be discreet, chaste, keepers at home, good, obedient to their own husbands, that the Word of God be not blasphemed." Titus 2:3-5*

These things are what you are to be learning and what you are to be discussing with others. These things are what God's young ladies are commanded to be doing.

You are not married now, but you should be focusing on learning to be a good wife. Now is the time to learn these things, not after you are married! And what better way to help instill and seal these things in your heart, but to be able to converse with other young ladies like yourself. And not only with the young ladies, but with your older sisters in the Lord, just as this Scripture teaches.

Finding Topics of Interest

Finding topics of interest to talk with others shouldn't be too difficult considering all the things there are to do if you are female! There are endless projects that you might have found. Such as making different jellies; cross stitch and whether you like working with one string or two; different cleansers you have discovered right in your very home, such as vinegar to clean with; or discussing an interesting article you have read in school. Remember that you are to encourage others in Christian girlhood and womanhood, and that any seemingly trivial piece of information is worthwhile, when trying to lift up others. You can also talk the Scriptures, but remember to stay off subjects that might be controversial and that should be left to a Bible Study or Church Meeting with the men in control. This stops many unpleasant disputes that may arise over a certain passage. Women should be kind and gentle towards one another, not disputing over words in anger.

Practice Talking Topics With Family and Friends

There are many families that have never learned to talk with one another. This is so very sad, for God has given families as a special gift. Children are a blessing from the Lord and God has given them to be trained and nurtured by loving parents.

There is no better place to learn how to discuss topics than with your family. If your family hasn't yet discovered this wonderful art, talk with your parents and ask them if you could start doing this today!

Many families use dinner time to talk about things that they have learned or experiences that they have had throughout the day. If you are just learning to converse, simply start by telling about something that you have read that day in school.

There was one young girl who was very quiet, and very shy, and it was very difficult for her to talk to others. Her mother simply had her say one thing that she had done that day. At first all she would say was, "I did my school." But the next week she would say, "I read in my English book that God says words are the basis of the Scriptures and that it is important that we learn to read them." Then the next week she would soon be talking even more about interesting topics in her readers!

Be a Very Good Listener

There is one important thing to always remember when you are talking with someone... If you can't think of anything to say, simply ask about them, and be genuinely concerned with the person you are speaking to!

This is Biblical! Do you remember what James told us? We are to be QUICK TO HEAR!!!! SLOW TO SPEAK!!!!

To be a good listener and a good conversationalist, you must also remember to stop thinking about yourself! Think about the other person you are talking to, and make it your duty to put them at ease. They might be just as uncomfortable at making conversation as you. In fact, always assume that people are nervous, and make it your pleasure to make them feel comfortable. Think of others, not yourself.

When you are a good listener, people will always be inclined to relax and talk.

Remember, always become genuinely interested in others and make yourself forget about YOU!

A List of Things to Avoid

There are some things to avoid when speaking to others:

~Do not talk too much about yourself.
~Do not exalt yourself or be a braggart.
~Do not interrupt others when they are talking. Let them finish.
~Do not be too familiar.
~Do not ever use coarse language or slang when speaking.
~Do not gossip or talk about others.
~Do not be sarcastic.
~Do not embarrass people.
~Do not talk down to others.
~Don't compete with other people's stories...

****
Discussion:

~Why is it important to be knowledgable regarding interests of womanhood?
~When speaking, what is the reason behind our words? (We are to be an encouragement to others!)
~Name some topics of interest that you could talk to others about. With older women? With girls your age? With a grand father?
~Are you shy? (Meaning that you get embarrassed when talk ing with others or don't know what to say?)
~What is the best thing to remember to talk about if you can't remember anything to say? (Ask questions about the other person.)
~What are some things to remember when listening?
~What is important to remember regarding other people? (That they might be nervous talking to you, and that you are to try to put them at ease by being more concerned with them, than with yourself.)
~How do you put others "at ease"?
~Name some things to avoid when talking with others.

Chapter Sixteen

THE DANGERS OF LAZINESS

I'm sure that you have heard of "being lazy" before, but do you know exactly what that means? According to the dictionary "laziness" is defined as the following:

1. A person who is resistant to work or exertion.
2. Disposed to idleness.
3. Slothful.
4. Slow-moving.
5. Sluggish.
6. Conducive to languor or indolence.
7. Depicted as reclining or lying on its side.

We all might feel like some of these things, sometimes. For example, in the summer sometimes it is "too hot to work"; but, this is not being lazy. A lazy person is someone who dislikes work and doesn't want to do it.

Someone who doesn't like to work is going to have a difficult time following God, because God likes work! Did you know that God created us to work six days? Yes! We are then given one day to rest!

Some people say that resting one day a week is legalistic. But one thing to remember is that God created a day of rest before He gave the Law. He created the day of rest when He made the world. It has always been this way for those that follow God and His ways.

"And God blessed the seventh day, and sanctified it; because that

in it He had rested from all His work which God created and made." Genesis 2:3

Did you know that in the beginning, even before the fall of Adam, that God created Adam to work? He was to "keep" and "dress" which meant to tend, work, take care of, the Garden of Eden. This was to be Adam's job.

"And the Lord God took the man, and put him into the garden of Eden to dress it and to keep it." Genesis 2:15

Some people believe that the "curse of God" after the fall was work. This is not so. Work was a blessing and gave a purpose for man. God worked, and then He rested. God worked six days and then rested the last day.

The problem in our society today is that most people want to do things that "make them feel good". They only want to live in pleasures upon this earth.

The sad thing is that because worldly parents don't really know how to work, they don't know how to teach their children to work. Society then will continue to get worse and worse.

But you as a believer in Christ will take pleasure in work as the Scriptures teach us! God has created you to do work. You will never have to say "I'm bored" in a haughty tone, because there is always something to do. There is always some way that you can be useful.

A Lazy Girl Will Grow Into a Lazy Mother & Wife

There was once a young girl who was born into a family that had quite a bit of money. The mother worked outside the home and had a housekeeper in to do all the cleaning and caring of the home because she had no time to do it.

The children in this family never had to pick up after themselves because the housekeeper did it for them. Because nothing was required of them, they simply lived a full life of pleasure. They watched television, they played their Nintendos, they talked on the phone with their friends, but never once were they taught to help.

The young girl in this family grew up. She found a young man who was raised the same way that she had been raised and married.

Because she had never been brought up to keep a home, she never knew that it was her duty to keep it clean, and to care for her home. Both she and her husband threw their clothing on the floor, expecting someone else to pick it up for them. Because neither would do so, their home soon became filthy, with piles of dishes in the kitchen, with dirty laundry covering the floors, and a terrible odor started emanating from their little habitation.

They would try to pick it up when it became more than they could bear, but soon it would be back in its same state.

Needless to say, this sad story is a very common tale of newlyweds today.

Because young ladies are not taught to work and to do the important duties of running a home, many marriages are in a total state of chaos.

What is even more terrifying is that these young couples are having children, and their children are going to be even worse than they are!

This is why it is so important for you to learn the honor of hard work.

"The hand of the diligent shall bear rule; but the slothful shall be under tribute." Proverbs 12:24

"The slothful man roasteth not that which he took in hunting; but the substance of a diligent man is precious." Proverbs 12:17

Have you ever been so lazy that you will not even take care of things that you have purchased? There are many children out there who are given toys that cost much money and they are so slothful that they don't even take care of these items. They leave them lying around their rooms and are not taught to even pick up what they have been playing with. This is not pleasing to God. We are required to be diligent in all things. This is pleasing to God. The Scriptures command us to do "all things as unto the Lord."

Laziness is Dishonoring to God

We are commanded to serve as if the Lord Jesus was right next to us, watching. And in fact, He is!

"Whatsoever thy hand findeth to do , do it with thy might; for there is no work, nor device, nor knowledge, nor wisdom, in the grave, whither thou goest." Ecclesiastic 9:10

We are only given a short time here on earth. Everything that we do and everything that we say we shall give an account for. The Bible tells us in 2 Corinthians 5:10 "We must all appear before the judgment seat of Christ; that every one may receive the things done in his body; according to that he hath done, whether it be good or bad."

This is why we must not be idle. This is a sin against the very life God has given you. We mock God when we live on this earth for pleasures.

Luke 8:14 tells us that the seed which fell among thorns are they, which, when they have heard, go forth, and are choked with cares and riches and pleasures of this life, and bring no fruit to perfection.

You might wish to study and truly think about the following Scriptures. God tells us in His Word how important it is to not live in idleness and pleasures.

"He that loveth pleasure shall be a poor man; he that loveth wine

and oil shall not be rich." Proverbs 21:17

"She looketh well to the ways of her household, and eateth not the bread of idleness." Proverbs 31:27

One thing that idleness brings with it is the problem of being a busybody. A busybody is a person who, because of idleness, meddles or pries into the business or affairs of others.

"For even when we were with you, this we commanded you, that if any would not work, neither should he eat. For we hear that there are some which walk among you disorderly, working not at all, but are busybodies. Now them that are such we command and exhort by our Lord Jesus Christ, that with quietness they work, and eat their own bread." 2 Thess. 3:10-11

"Withal they learn to be idle, wandering about from house to house; and not only idle, but tattlers also and busybodies, speaking things which they ought not." 1 Timothy 5:13

As young women in Christ, your main goal should be to keep yourself busy, to mind your own business, and to live a life useful to God's Kingdom. We are to be busy regarding the matters of the Kingdom!

****

Discussion:

~What is LAZINESS?
~Describe in length the difference between living a life of pleasure and ease, and living a life that works six days and rests one. Try to make a parallel of people living their lives for Christ and then living their lives according to the social customs of this world. What are the differences. Make a list and the see if you might have any of these tendencies. Take them to the Lord in prayer.

Chapter Seventeen

WOMEN'S WORK

There was a movement many years ago called "The Feminist Movement". It took just a few idle women, whose husband's had quite a bit of money, to start printing literature and traveling to our nation's capital, to change what the world then called "Women's Work".

They said that all women were "slaves" in their homes and that they no longer wanted to be homemakers. They wanted to become equal with men, or rather, they wanted to BECOME men! They had become discontent with "home life" and wanted to join the work force.

Now, many years later, most of the women of today were raised with the ideas that were held by these very same women. Because of their political lobbying, they were able to have these philosophies taught as "education" in the public school system. Their idea of banning, or getting rid of, the idea of "traditional women's work", and their goal to get women out of the home and into the work force in order to "be equal or the same as men", has become the "norm" of our society today.

But God has a different plan for you, my young friend. He has called women to a very honorable and esteemed position. It is that wonderful title of "mother"!

The Young Girl's Future Hope

Most likely, you will some day grow up and become a wife and mother. Did you know that God has created you with this desire in your heart? Throughout history, young girls have always played with dolls, and have imitated their mothers in playing "house". Why do you think that they inherently gravitate to this type of play? Because it is how God has created us.

Did you know that God has given His female creation the opportunity to contribute to His Kingdom through raising children for Him?

Don't be deceived into thinking that the false teaching of leaving your home and centering your life around a career is higher than the calling of wife and mother. There is a wonderful hope in God's calling of women.

No worldly job in the work force can even begin to compare to the joy of raising godly sons and daughters, or the responsibility of instilling God's morals and values upon them. How wonderful to be able to train them spiritually and physically, and to actually be able to give yourself away to these young men and women of tomorrow!

However, what has happened in our society is that mothers may be having children physically, but they are neglecting to train their own children and are passing this important responsibility to godless educational systems. When mothers stopped mothering, the whole world was thrown into chaos, and children have become *orphans* in their own families.

What will a *career* mother say to God on judgment day, "God, I became the president of the company I was working for, and made more money than any other woman employed there."

And God will say, "You have sold your children's souls for money and a career. You have regarded the gift of children I blessed you with as unimportant and a hindrance. My blessings have become curses as you sought the world rather than the Word."

Dearest sister, if you are seeking God, you will know to seek after the hope of His calling. That of womanhood in Him, not of the world.

The Future Young Mother

We've just talked a bit about the importance of motherhood. The attitude and perception of motherhood is something to look at now. If you look on motherhood as something that is wonderful and a blessing, then you will be a mother that is wonderful and a blessing to her children.

If you look upon motherhood as something that takes up your time and is self-consuming and a hindrance; then your mothering will be hindered, and you will raise children that are self-absorbed and are unruly.

As a mother, you will raise what you are. Your children will be little mirrors of you. They will hold your perceptions, your attitudes and your philosophies of life.

But this is where the joy of Christ comes in. As you are growing in Christ, your children help to perfect you! It's true!

"Notwithstanding she shall be saved in childbearing, if they continue in faith and charity and holiness with sobriety." 1 Timothy 2:15

This Scripture is talking about women being "saved" through childbearing. Some people have taken this wrong and thought that by the act of having children you will get into heaven. If this were so, then why do people in other countries have 14 to 21 children and still worship another God? Are they saved through the bearing of these children? No.

According to the original Greek word, "saved", or "sozo" in Greek, means:

~Deliver.
~Protect.
~Heal.
~Preserve.

~Save self.
~Do well.
~Be made whole.

The word "childbearing", or "teknogonia", means:

~Bear children.
~Parent.
~Mother.
~The performance of maternal duties.

In other words, this Scripture is telling us that as we become a mother, and perform our maternal duties, God will deliver us, protect us, heal us, preserve us, save us from ourselves, have us do well, and we will be made whole!

On the other hand, if we do not perform our maternal duties, and if we neglect to be a mother, we won't be able to be as complete as God would have us be.

There are some who would argue this Scripture and say, "But there are some women who are childless. Through no fault of their own they cannot have children. Are you saying these women are never going to be complete in Christ?"

You don't have to have children yourself in order to have children. Even the Scriptures command us:

"Pure religion and undefiled before God and the Father is this, To visit the fatherless and widows in their affliction, and to keep himself unspotted from the world." James 1:27

We are commanded to take care of orphans. What a wonderful way for the childless to obtain children!

You must be careful that you never listen to the world and its thoughts towards children. Today people think that it is wrong to have more than two children. This is not God's truth.

Having children is a blessing. You are a blessing! As a child, you are a good thing! You are a precious gift from God, a present to your parents.

Psalms 127:3 "Lo children are an heritage of the Lord; and the fruit of the womb is his reward.

And the Scripture then continues...

Psalms 127:4-5 "As arrows are in the hand of a mighty man; so are children of the youth. Happy is the man that hath his quiver full of them; they shall not be ashamed, but they shall speak with the enemies in the gate."

You must teach your children the importance of motherhood. It can't be stressed enough, that you must have the perception towards motherhood that God does. Then you will grow up to pass this on to your own children.

"My son, hear the instruction of thy father, and forsake not the law of thy mother." Proverbs 1:8

"A foolish man despiseth his mother." Proverbs 15:20

Motherhood is to be honored. There is no higher calling!

The Need for Order and Organization

We have just been studying how becoming a mother is a blessed gift from God. Now we are going to talk a bit about becoming an "organized and orderly mother".

What type of person are you? Do you carefully fold all your clothes and place them neatly in your drawer? Do you have a place for everything and everything in its place? Or are you one who throws items on the ground thinking that you'll pick them up later? Only later seems to get later and later?

If you have difficulty being orderly, you can learn this good quality. It's deciding to change and then doing so through prayer and through Christ's strength.

*"**Order my steps in thy Word;** and let not any iniquity have dominion over me." Psalms 119:133*

The Scriptures tell us to line everything we do up with the Word of God. We should pray each morning and ask God to help us with our duties. He will give us direction!

"Let all things be done decently and in order." 1 Corinthians 14:40

The need for order and organization in your home cannot be overemphasized. You must learn now to become orderly. Take a look around your home. Has your mother organized her house? For example, you probably won't find bathroom supplies in a bedroom, or kitchen supplies in the bathroom! This is an example of organization.

When learning how to be orderly, you have to start sorting *like* objects. It's just like mathematics! You can't add together *unlike objects* in math. You can't add dogs and oranges. But you can add oranges and oranges. We use this same principle in becoming orderly in the home.

In your home now, you will learn to place all bathroom objects in the bathroom. In the girl's room you will only place the girl's belongings. You will only place boy's items in the boy's rooms. You find a place for kitchen items and only place them in the kitchen.

Learning to be orderly is very simple.

One thing to watch out for is if you have a tendency to be a *pack rat...* A *pack rat* is one who gathers anything and never throws it away. They even collect trash and stuff it anywhere where there is room.

Always ask yourself, "Is this a something that I need?" when you are cleaning your room. If you have something that is absolutely useless, but you are just hanging onto it for junk's sake, make yourself throw it away. If you absolutely want to remember it, take a picture of the object and then throw it away. Pictures are easy to store, but objects of no use are considered trash, regardless of how much you may be attached to it.

"For though I be absent in the flesh, yet am I with you in the spirit, joying and ***beholding your order,*** *and the steadfastness of your faith in Christ." Colossians 2:5*

Being orderly will also bring you joy and peace. When you are not orderly, you will not be able to be competent in your homemaking. An attitude of hopelessness and helplessness arises. Then the mother becomes discouraged because her house is out of order.

This is why it is so important for you to learn now how to be orderly and organized.

It's not very hard. Ask the Lord for guidance on showing you and helping you to get rid of things that you do not need. Then ask Him to help you become creative in placing things that you do need in a proper place.

It is a wonderful thing to be tidy and orderly in your home. Start with the home you are in now so that your home in the future will be easy to maintain because you have developed those skills at an early age.

Goal Planning

The next step to becoming an "orderly and organized mother", is to learn how to set goals for yourself. It's called *setting your priori-*

ties. In other words, you must decide what should be done first. Learn now to start your day with prayer before you even get out of bed. Ask your Heavenly Father to order your day in what He would have you do.

Try to make a list every morning. Have this list contain six things that you would like to do. For example, your *to do* list might look like the following:

1. Bible Reading
2. School
3. Clean room
4. Write thank you notes
5. Dust house
6. Tend baby brother for one hour

This is just an example, but it might help you to get an idea of what you do in one day.

Be aware of TIME STEALERS. These are things such as: sewing to excess, talking too long on the telephone, window shopping, and other time consuming things. This doesn't mean that you can't ever do these things, but you should be mindful of them and not allow it to happen too often.

Sometimes you may fall way short of your list, but don't feel as if you have failed. Simply add them to the next day's list, and maybe you can accomplish them that day.

"The steps of a good man are ordered by the Lord; and he delighteth in his way. Though he fall, he shall not be utterly cast down; for the Lord upholdeth him with His hand." Psalms 37:23

Another way to make sure that you are able to reach your goals each day is to not make them too hard to attain. Keep them simple. Also remember, the less you have to worry about materialistically, the easier your home life will be. If you learn now not to be a hoarder of worldly objects, you will find life easier when you are married. The more things you have, the more work you will have to maintain those *things*. You can have nice items, but just have a few. Learn to only have what you need. That is the secret of living a fulfilled and contended life in Christ!

****

Discussion:

~What does the world tell young women to do? (Go to col lege, get a degree and then have a career.)
~Where do children fit into this?
~What does the Scriptures teach regarding women? Where are they to be? (Titus 2:5 "...To be discreet, chaste, **keepers at home**, good, obedient to their own husbands, that the Word of God be not blasphemed.")
~What is the most important calling a woman will have? (To be a wife and mother.)
~Why is it more important than a career?
~What does the saying, "the hand the rocks the cradle is the hand that rules the world", mean? (That the rulers of this world are brought up with the philosophies of their mothers.)
~Explain what it means to be "saved through childbearing".
~Why is it important that you learn to be orderly now?
~What does the Bible tell you about orderliness?
~What will your future home be like if you are NOT orderly?
~What will it be like if you ARE orderly?
~Describe some of the goals you must set in your own life.
~Describe your daily goals.

Read: Proverbs 29:18
(Where there is no vision, the people perish; but he that keepeth the law, happy is he.)

~Explain this in your own words. What does that have to do with goals? What happens if you don't have a goal?
~What is our TRUE goal? (HEAVEN!!!!!!)

Chapter Eighteen

WHAT ARE YOUR FEMALE RESPONSIBILITIES IN LIFE?

God has created you to be a wonderful female in Him! With this comes the role of nurturing others and caring for the belongings that He will give you in your life.

God has given specific duties He requires of us in order to be able to care for our loved ones and place where our loved ones live.

Some people call this duty "homemaking", which is a wonderful word. There are many "houses", but it takes the special touch of a female in Christ to "make one a home". This is why "homemaking", and "homemaker" are the most important jobs in all the world.

You can have children and place them in a house, but, that doesn't necessarily mean that you will have a "home" being taken care of by a caring "mother". It takes a loving mother who is there training her children, who God looks upon as a true "mother". It takes a loving woman to care for, create, and make a "home". This is what God has told us to be. We are to be "keepers of the home"!

The following topics are the basics of what our duties should be throughout our lives. This is very simplified, but it will give you a place to start.

Cleaning Skills

Let's start with your room. Is your room clean? With that I don't mean just picked up. Is the dust and dirt totally swept from your room? If you haven't yet learned this skill, it's a very easy one to attain. The wonderful thing is that when you have learned to conquer the cleaning of your own room, you will be able to handle a whole house!

~Start with your floor. Are there objects on the floor? Remove anything on the floor and place it on your bed.

~Remove all excess items on your dressers and bookshelves. Place them on your bed.

~Take inventory. Your room should be spotless by now. That is, everything that shouldn't be on the floor, dresser and bookshelves, you can now find on your bed. Put everything up that is on your bed. If you do not have a spot for something, give it away to Goodwill or to a friend.

~Vacuum first! Never EVER dust and then vacuum. Even though the vacuum is supposed to suck up all the dirt and dust from your floor, it still exhausts minuscule particles of dust. This is why you always vacuum and then dust. You start vacuuming by getting the attachment for edges. It is the long skinny one. Go all the way around your room and get every single dust bunny around the edges. Make sure that you go under your furniture, also, with the T attachment. Next, vacuum the entire floor. Move furniture that is not too heavy and vacuum under it, also.

~Dust all wood furniture. Use a cheesecloth, slightly moistened, followed with a dry cloth, commercial dust cloth, or feather duster. Spray or dab lemon oil, or some type of furniture oil, on the dust cloth. This protects the wood and will cause your wood furniture to last hundreds of years. Get all crevasses. Take off items in order to dust and after dusting these items too, replace nicely. Always make it nicer than it was before!

~Clean glass and mirrors with some type of ammonia cleaner. We put glass on top of our wood dressers and so we clean them till they shine. Our sparkling secret is to always dry and clean the glass and mirrors with newspapers once the cleaner is sprayed on to the surface. It's amazing how clean they get!

~Change your sheets! This is something that many young girls forget to do. You should change your sheets once a week. Launder your sheets in very hot water with some Downy, or other fabric softener, in the rinse cycle and your whole room will smell fresh and clean!

Remember the art of always doing things *femininely*? Always emphasizing the difference between being female from male? Keep that in mind when you are cleaning. Remember to add feminine touches to your room. Have soft pillows in your room, learn to crochet some doilies to place around on top of your dressers and bookshelves. On top of them place a vase of fresh flowers.

Last, but not least, always go the extra mile, as Christ has taught us. Do everything as unto the Lord... even your cleaning. Don't do a job half way. Do it more than all the way. Put your heart into all that you do.

Be thankful for every object that you have as you are taking care of your earthly possessions. Be thankful that you have a room to clean and care for!

Organizing Skills

In the previous chapter we talked a bit about becoming orderly and organized. The reason why we are talking about it again, is that in order for you to truly be able to keep a room clean (and then your home in the future), you must be organized.

Imagine a room where there are tons and tons of objects scattered everywhere. You wouldn't know where to begin! You can't clean with messes blocking your way. How can you dust wood furniture if there are hundreds of items on top of it? You can't! Then the dust collects and soon it will turn into sticky grime. Not to mention that it will also cause allergies in your home. There is nothing more terrible than sickness caused from being dirty.

Imagine if you are not organized in your kitchen. You have lots of food; but, because everything is not organized in the pantry, you can't find the food and it becomes a chaotic catastrophe! You have groceries, but don't know what is there, because they are scattered all over the cupboards.

Being organized is the way to stop stress and tension. It will bring a peace and a gentleness to your feminine being.

Mending, Fixing & Sewing Skills

One of the most important money saving skills that you can develop is that of mending and sewing. It is also one of the easiest ways in which you can have feminine and modest clothing.

Have you gone to the clothing stores lately? The world does not cater to feminine women in the area of modest clothing. They offer tight, straight dresses which reveal rather than conceal a woman's figure. The colors are dark and manly, and there are very few items available that are soft and lovely.

This is where the fine art of sewing comes in!

You can go to your fabric store at the end of each season and purchase quality cotton for less than $1.50 a yard. We usually find lovely cottons for .99 cents. We can make a beautiful, feminine creation for less than $10; and, also be assured that it is a wholesome, modest dress for a young lady representing Christ to wear.

It is so important for a young girl to learn to sew. Not only will she be able to sew clothes at a fraction of the cost of store bought; but, she will be able to develope a skill that will be useful for her future family.

Not only can she sew clothing, but she can sew baby clothes, baby sheets, curtains, purses, diaper bags, tablecloths, and more! The list is endless. I knew of a young woman who wanted to give a present to her older sister when she had a baby. She knew that her sister had been looking for flannel baby sheets for the crib; but, she had been unsuccessful in finding one. This frugal and thoughtful young woman went to the fabric store, purchased four yards of flannel for $8, and sewed a wonderful set of flannel baby sheets that would have cost $28 for two, if you could even find them.

Often, they are only available through an expensive, all cotton, baby catalog!

To learn to sew, go to the library and find a beginner's *how-to* book. There are many to choose from. We enjoyed Simplicity's beginner sewing instructional book. Start with a simple project such as a tablecloth. Then try curtains with ruffles. Next, try a pillow. When you feel you are ready, try to make a skirt. Soon you will be sewing everything in no time!

Cooking Skills

Have you ever heard the saying, "The way to a man's heart is through his tummy?" This means, if you are going to be a wife and mother some day, you had better learn to be a great cook!

There have been so many Christian men who have married wives and then found out they couldn't cook. What sorrow for these men. But there have also been men who have married young ladies *because of their* culinary skills (not to mention they also loved her) and they are the happiest of creatures.

Being a good cook, requires that you not only can create food which tastes good, but, making sure that it is also nourishing to your family. That is the secret of a good cook

Here are four important rules to always remember:

1) Cook *healthy* food.
2) Make it *look* good as well as taste good. (Garnish!)
3) Make it *smell* good.
4) Cook for your families' taste, not your own.

What do you remember about your Granny's cooking? I picture mine in the kitchen with her apron on, caring for a pan of fried onions, the sizzling aroma beckoning anyone within a mile to come into the house for something that was surely melt-in-the-mouth ambrosia. My eyes closed in pleasure, my nose up in the air breathing in the mouth watering fragrance, and then I'd turn and watch her scurry over to another pot to stir the vegetables; opening the oven as she checked the pot roast. Now THAT was cooking! What made her cooking so memorable was also the smell!

Did you know that recently there was some research done regarding men's favorite smell. Did you know what it was? No, it wasn't expensive French perfume; it wasn't light flowery scents... It was the smell of APPLE PIE!!!! 99% of men who took this test claimed that their favorite scent in the whole world was apple pie.

Remember to always bake something that will leave that homemade fragrance in the air for your children and your husband to remember in their old age. Cinnamon, spices, onions, apple pie, cookies, bread... These are the makings of memories. It's not just the eating of food. That's what is missing in all the prepackaged foods. The preparation is missing, and with that, the smell of home cooked food.

Start your cooking now! It's easy. Here's what to do:

~Go collect some interesting books from your local library.
~Go through them and find one recipe that you think you might like to try.
~Make an item list and take it to your mother. See what you have on hand and what you don't have, make a grocery list.
~Purchase everything you need.
~Start following the recipe AFTER you have read it through com pletely.

You will be surprised at what you can create! It will be fun and it will also be a help to your mother. Once you become really good, she will probably even let you start cooking some of the meals for your family!....

Teaching Skills - You Will Someday be a Teacher!

What is a teacher? It is someone that teaches other people about a subject. Have you ever taught someone how to play a game? How to do anything? If so, then you too are a teacher!

When you grow up and have children of your own, you are automatically a teacher. In fact, a mother is the most important teacher of all. Knowing you probably will end up becoming a mother and a teacher when you are older, you need to be aware of teaching skills.

Here are some things to remember:

~Never lose your temper when you are explaining something to someone and when they don't understand right away.

~Always talk kindly when explaining.

~When you must explain over and over, do not get exasperated, but remember the Scripture which says you must forgive 70 x 70, and then remember not to start counting!

~Follow the "True Love" chapter.

~Always look for things that God is teaching you now and explain them to others. This way you will always be learning new things to encourage others in the Lord.

~Everything you learn now will eventually be passed on to your children.

~Remember that worldly knowledge and godly knowledge are two different things. You can be wise about all things of the world and still be unknowledgeable in the ways of God.

~Seek God first and His ways and all the rest will be added to you.

"But seek ye first the kingdom of God, and His righteousness; and all these things shall be added unto you." Matthew 6:33

Money Skills

Handling money with true frugality is one of the best gifts a young girl can learn! She will truly be a blessing to her husband as he will place his hard earned money into her very capable hands.

"The heart of her husband doth safely trust in her, so that he shall have no need of spoil." Proverbs 31:11

The word "spoil" in this scripture is the Hebrew word "shalal". It means to plunder, fall, make self a prey.

In other words, this scripture means that this man can safely trust his wife to not bring him to poverty. She will not prey off of her husband and want more than he can provide. She will be one in whom he can trust in every way.

She will not go out and purchase a coat that costs thousands of dollars and come home parading it in front of her husband and drop the information that she simply "charged" it on his credit card.

She will not spend his money on things they do not need, on worthless ornaments of expense.

There are many women who have brought their families much sorrow because they have wanted to live above their means. What does "living above one's means" really mean? Well, it means they see people all around them who look as if they have more material goods, people who are living in bigger houses, people who are driving expensive cars, people who wear designer clothes that cost 50 times more than just decent, functional clothing. They watch these people and then they want to have what they have.

Did you know that this is breaking one of the Ten Commandments? It is breaking the commandment "Thou shalt NOT covet." That is wanting what someone else has and it is wrong.

As a young lady, you must learn first to live within the means that you father provides for you. You must have a contented and thankful heart for what he is able to give to you and never want more.

Do not spend the money that your parents give to you heedlessly. Don't spend money on candy and pleasures of your flesh. If you do this now, you will grow up to have a difficult time not buying items for the pleasures of your flesh when you are a woman with a husband and children.

Here are some suggestions to follow regarding money:

~Learn to be frugal.
~Never be extravagant.
~Try to always save half of what you are given.
~Do not give in to fleshly temptations of materialism.
~Buy the best clothing, or make the best clothing, on sale, and take care of them.
~Have certain clothing for certain functions. For example, have washing clothes, work clothes, church clothes, day clothes, and sleeping clothes.
~Do not hoard clothing. This is costly and fleshly.
~Never buy anything that you have not thought about buying for at least two days. This stops spontaneous buying!
~Never buy anything that you are not sure of. If you aren't quite sure if it looks right, or if you really want to eat it... don't buy it!
~Do not shop at Dollar Stores unless you have first made a list. Money slips through your hands because you are buying "DEALS". These are usually frivolous expenditures.
~When you go shopping with your mother, beware of using coupons unless they are products you normally buy. Unnecessary items are usually bought in this way.

The Bible says that the parents "kept" their daughters until they were given away in marriage. They then became the responsibility of their new husband. When your parents give you money, be aware that this is a blessing and a gift from them. Money is hard to come by, and, you should always have a grateful heart that they would give you a portion.

It is also a great blessing when a husband will trust part of his income into the hands of the wife. She has the God-given duty to spend that money wisely.

Someday you will also have that important responsibility. Learn now to treat money wisely so that you will be a blessing and a joy to your husband; you then will be able to teach your children the art of frugality!

TENDER LOVING DEEDS

The Bible tells us that we are to be full of good works. What are works? The definition means:

1. Toil.
2. As an effort or occupation.
3. An Act.
4. A deed.
5. Doing.
6. Labor.
7. Work.

In other words, we need to toil towards a good occupation. For women, that is homemaking and mothering. We need to do good acts or good deeds. We need to do good. We need to labor well, and do good works!

"That they do good, that they be rich in good works, ready to distribute, willing to communicate; laying up in store for themselves a good foundation against the time to come, that they may lay hold on eternal life." 1 Timothy 6:18

When we toil and work for the Lord, we need to focus not on this life, but on the life to come. We are to encourage one another towards good works.

"And let us consider one another to provoke unto love and to good works." Hebrews 10:24

Our duties, done unto the Lord, are our good works. We are to fill our lives with serving others. That is what it is to be a mother and a wife... We also live a life of doing good works because we love God, and, want to live a life pleasing to Him. It's not our works that get us into Heaven; but, our love of God that causes us to obey Him.

"Blessed are they that do His commandments, that they may have the right to the tree of life, and may enter in through the gates into the city." Revelation 22:14

****

Discussion:

~What is a "homemaker"? (A woman who makes a house a home.)
~Discuss the difference between throwing a house together and putting your heart into it...
~Why is it important to have a clean home?
~How can you learn to clean a whole house? (You start with just one room, your own.)
~Write down a plan of action on how you are going to tackle your room.
~Is your room organized? Are your drawers organized? Have you de-junked your belongings? (If you haven't, you should plan on cleaning your room before you clean anything else.
~The next step is to do it a little bit each day, so it won't get dirty again.)
~Why are all mothers teachers?
~List some things to remember when you are instructing others.
~What is frugality?
~What does the scriptures say about spending more than our fathers or our husbands earn? (Proverbs 31)
~How are we to be rich? (Not money! We are to be rich in good deeds.)
~Memorize 1 Timothy 6:18

Chapter Nineteen

HOSPITALITY

What do you think of when you hear the word hospitality? Do you picture smiles, friendship, and warmth of a home? Do you think of family, friends, and fellowship?

One of the arts of being a Christian woman is that of hospitality. More than an art, it is an act of heart, for hospitality is graciousness that comes from within. It is the willingness to host other people and to serve and make them feel welcome in your home.

"...distributing to the necessity of saints; given to hospitality..." Romans 12:13

This is a Scripture commanding us to be hospitable. What does it mean to be hospitable? The Strong's Concordance tells us that it means:

1) Being hospitable.
2) Entertain strangers.
3) Fond of guests.
4) Given to and a lover of hospitality.

The dictionary tells us that hospitable means:

1) Welcoming guests with warmth and generosity.
2) Fond of entertaining.
3) Well disposed towards strangers.
4) Having an open and charitable mind.
5) Receptive.

Hospitality means:

1) The act or practice of, or a tendency toward being hospitable.
2) An instance of being hospitable.

We are called to be ambassadors for Christ. This is part of hospitality. An ambassador is an authorized messenger or representative. When we show hospitality to others we have the wonderful opportunity to open our lives and give them a view into a home where Christ reigns. He is the King, and we are His representatives. How wonderful to be able to represent a Christ-centered home and family to others!

!

Entertaining Strangers

"Be not forgetful to entertain strangers; for thereby some have entertained angels unaware." Hebrews 13:2

In this Scripture we are encouraged to invite people that we do not know into our homes. We are told that people have entertained angels this way without even knowing it!

By "entertaining", do we mean that they danced for angels, or sang for angels, without knowing it? No, entertaining here means "to be a host"; "to lodge"; and the last definition says, "to think it strange". Isn't that funny? But there are many people in our society who think it very strange to host strangers. They refuse to have anyone they do not know into their homes. They are afraid of strangers, and will only invite those people whom they know well into their home.

God has called us to be kind and hospitable to others. Someone once said, "A home without visitors is not a perfect home." Did you know that having visitors means that we have contact with other people? This causes us to sharpen our beliefs and it also gives us an opportunity to spread the light He has given us to others.

Did you know that people who do not have other people over eventually become a world unto their own? It is true. They become selfish and withdrawn. This is the opposite of what the Bible tells us to be. The Word of God tells us to be a "light" or "salt". How can we do that if we withdraw and never open our homes for others to come into?

A family which chooses not to invite other people over, eventually cuts off all connections of true fellowship. Church is fine, but it is not the same as inviting other people over for food and friendship. A home like this becomes a prison within it's own boundaries.

When families do not fellowship with others, they have a tendency to become cold. They start lacking sympathy or kindness towards anyone who does not think as they do. Sadly, when they keep to themselves because they are not able to show hospitality to others, they become mean-spirited, and this is passed on to their children. These children start to show attitudes of self-righteousness and arrogance, which is such a shame.

God has told us to fellowship with others.

"And let us consider one another to provoke unto love and to good works; not forsaking the assembling of ourselves together, as the manner of some is; but exhorting one another; and so much the more, as ye see the day approaching." Hebrews 10:24-25

This word "assembling" is the Greek word #1997, episunago, which means to collect, meeting, gathering together. Many people believe that this means the formal "church". Others believe that it means the more informal and intimate "Bible Study" of like-minded believers in the home.

Whichever you happen to believe, it means that we should be

more than willing to meet with other believers; and, what better way than to open your heart and home in order to fellowship with others!

Opening Your Heart and Home

As Christ's, we must never be afraid of anyone. We need to have the heart that each person we meet might be made into a friend in Christ. This is a much better way to act than to treat each stranger as if they were an intruder.

The best way to treat others is to never treat them as though you were in a hurry to be done with them, but as though you have all the time in the world to cultivate them, and speak of the hope you have in Christ. To not treat others this way is to harm yourself. Our Heavenly Father would have us invite strangers to become friends by our treating them kindly.

When you have people over, you show that you are unselfish. Many people in this world today are so caught up with their own lives they never notice they are hurting people around who need God through His Son, Jesus Christ. There are many people who are lonely, and would give anything for a friendly smile or kind action. We are ambassadors of our King, and as such we must show that HE is hospitable to others!

When you meet other people, always be ready to give a sunny smile and to invite newly met strangers over to your home. You will send sunshine to the soul, and you will make other's hearts leap with hope as you have an opportunity to LIVE the Word in front of those who don't yet know the Savior.

All people long for friendly communication, and when people shun one another in our cold society of today, they pine and grow sick in their hearts. No wonder growing numbers of medical patients are diagnosed with depression.

Daniel Webster said, "We should make it a principle to extend the hand of fellowship to every man who discharges faithfully his duties and maintains good order, who manifests a deep interest in the general welfare of society, whose deportment is upright, and whose mind is intelligent, without stopping to ascertain whether he swings a hammer or draws a thread."

Many older people are saddened and discouraged at how mean our society has become. They have said that we are not social enough in the polite way. They say that we are not often at one another's houses. That we are especially negligent in the duty of having strangers over.

A dear sister in Christ told us the story of how she and her family moved to a new city in her state because of her husband's job, and so they were visiting churches. They went to four or five different places, and each time they were more discouraged than before.

No one talked to them; no one shook their hands. A few people would nod quickly at them, but no one took the time to come up and speak to them. Everyone seemed to be in a hurry to leave the buildings once the services were over. There were some people who were talking a bit, in a circle, but the circle was never opened to allow the new people in.

How awful that we have come to the place where we do not welcome newcomers and don't try to make their first visit as pleasant as possible. This is wrong. We have a duty as Christians to treat everyone as kind as possible, to try with everything in our being to influence others and show a kind consideration for their welfare.

Church is a wonderful place to be able to invite others over.

There was another sister who had a remarkable young lady in the Lord come up to her, her first time at an evening women's Bible Study, and invite her and her family over for lunch the following day! This dear sister still praises God for the kindness shown to her by this wonderful young lady and now she tries to also do this for others. They have made sound and fulfilling friendships in the Lord because of her being willing to open her home and heart to people!

Being hospitable doesn't mean that you are to be overly intimate with others. It doesn't mean that you share that which is personal or being indecently familiar with strangers or friends. It simply means that you are opening your home and giving of your heart through true Christian grace.

To be hospitable all you have to do is to:

~Invite someone over.

~Give them something to eat and drink.

~Have friendly conversation

~Give the feeling of kindness and goodwill through your tone of voice.

~Let the love of Christ reign throughout your chaste conversation.

In urging hospitality, we do not ignore the fact that there are many people to be found in every walk of life, you would as soon think of taking a serpent into the heart of your family as some people who infest society.

But this doesn't lessen the importance of hospitality! Just like you choose fruit, you are not required to eat good fruit and also the bad, the nutritious as well as the poisonous. No, you are to exercise good judgement!

So you are not required to be frank, openhearted, and sociable with villains, depraved and licentious people. To do this is to sink yourself to their level.

God will lead His people. You will know by the pulling of the Holy Spirit on your heart strings what you are to do. The Lord is truly a living Lord and speaks to our hearts and helps us today!

****

Discussion:

Read: Luke 14:12-14 *"Then said he also to him that bade him,*

When thou makest a dinner or a supper, call not thy friends, nor thy brethren, neither thy kinsmen, not thy rich neighbors; lest they also bid thee again, and a recompense be made thee. But when thou makest a feast, call the poor, the maimed, the lame, the blind; and thou shalt be blessed; for they cannot recompense thee; for thou shalt be recompensed at the resurrection of the dead."

~Who were they commanded to be hospitable towards? (Those that could not pay them back.)
~Have you ever heard people say, "We had them over, and it's their turn to have us back"? In light of this Scripture, is this a right attitude to have?
~What should our attitude be towards hospitality?
~Give your own definition of what hospitality means.
~How are we ambassadors?
~How does being an ambassador relate to being hospitable?
~What does the Scripture tell us regarding fellowship?
~When you open your heart and your home, are you becom ing vulnerable? (Yes! But we become vulnerable when we wake up each morning and place our feet on the floor! All of life is this way. But we are not to live our lives afraid. Rather, we are to live our lives in Christ, knowing that we are in the palm of God's hand, and that in our lives there is no such thing as an accident or a coincidence!)
~How do we help the lonely?
~Can families be lonely? (Yes! There are many families who attend churches every week, who enter in and then leave, never having truly talked with another person or having true fellowship with another believer.)
~How can you be hospitable as a young girl?
~Start a book of hospitality ideas for guests. Keep a plain, blank, notebook and copy recipes, house decorations, and creative guest ideas, neatly pasted in sections of it. You can refer to this homemade book, and add to it as you clip and paste from homemaking magazines!

Chapter Twenty

LAST BUT NOT LEAST

Many young girls today think that the ultimate goal in life is to be happy. This is a nice thought. We all want to be happy. The Bible tells us to have the joy of the Lord. But the difference between a girl who follows God and a girl who follows the world is in *the way* in which they obtain happiness!

The world will look around them at the pleasures of the world and think that those things will make them happy. For example, they believe that anything that will satisfy their flesh will bring them joy. Movies, the adoration of other people, becoming famous, dressing in the latest fashions, obsession with false beauty, and many other types of worldly cares are what they *think* brings them joy. They think that having money and obtaining worldly possessions is going to make them happy!

But this is such a lie from our enemy, the devil.

Remember when Satan brought Jesus up to a high point and was tempted by the devil?

" Then was Jesus led up of the spirit into the wilderness to be tempted of the devil... Then the devil taketh him up into an exceeding high mountain, and sheweth him all the kingdoms of the world, and the glory of them; and saith unto him, All these things will I give thee, if thou wilt fall down and worship me. Then saith Jesus unto him, Thou shalt worship the Lord thy God, and him only shalt thou serve. Then the devil leaveth him, and, behold, angels came and ministered unto him." Matthew 4:1+

We must remember that the glories of this world are simply

temptations from Satan, and when we live a life simply to pleasure ourselves, we are not able to live a life of service for our Heavenly Father.

2 Timothy warns us that in the last days men will be, *"Traitors, heady, high-minded,* ***lovers of pleasures more than lovers of God."*** *(2 Timothy 3:4)*

The Scriptures talk about the fact that once you accept Christ as your Savior, then you are a changed person. No longer will you want to live to pleasure your own self!

"For we ourselves also were sometimes foolish, disobedient, deceived, ***serving divers (different) lusts and pleasures****, living in malice and envy, hateful, and hating one another." Titus 3:3*

No, we are now of a different heart.

Our joy comes from being unselfish! True happiness comes from loving God with all of our hearts, all of our souls, and all of our minds. That is happiness!

Being Joyful

Have you ever thought about what "JOY" is? Joy means to be happy; it means to be full of gladness and having the ability to be content in every situation you are in.

Does this mean that if you are joyful you will never have any problems? Absolutely not! Our problems are from the Lord in that they work out His perfect will in our lives in order to perfect us. It is our joy in Christ that allows us to make it through the problems we will encounter in this life.

Are you joyful now? If not, perhaps you are living a life that is only self-fulfilling. The secret of living in the joy of the Lord is to live a life for others. We have talked a bit about this throughout the book, but this truth cannot be emphasized enough.

You will not find joy or happiness from chemicals or alcohol. You cannot buy all the entertainment systems in the world in order to obtain joy. This joy only comes from giving yourself away. Joy and happiness come to the person who lives their life for others.

Some people believe that they can't be happy because they live in the country. Some people believe they can't be happy because they live in the city! The truth of the matter is, even when they move, they are still unhappy, but yet will blame this unhappiness because of *where* they are, not because of *what* they are. The truth of it is, they are self-centered rather than Christ centered!

Pleasures versus the Joy of the Lord

We talked a bit about how some people believe that joy is the same thing as pleasure. This is a false thought. Pleasure is what makes our flesh feel good. Pleasure is what your carnal self lives for.

According to the dictionary, one definition was very interesting. It said:

~Pleasures are amusements, diversions, or other worldly enjoy -ments.
~Sensual gratification or indulgence.

Pleasures only come from fleshly desires and satisfy only the flesh.

On the other hand, joy & happiness, stem from within. They are *not* the result of earthly amusements, diversions or other worldly enjoyments.

Someone once said that pleasure comes from earthly amusements, while true joy comes from overcoming the flesh!

True joy will come from overcoming your flesh... Think of that! As you struggle through your day, think of the satisfaction you will have when that day is completed and you can go to God in prayer and be able to tell Him that you have accomplished what He willed for your life! That is joy!

Every time you have reached the goals you have set in regard towards your home and family duties, you should be joyful! What a blessed life and what a wonderful purpose we have as young women.

Seek God and His way, and you will truly find joy and peace!

The Happy Heart

We've come to the end of this book, and we pray that you have been encouraged towards true joy and happiness through learning about living a life of sacrifice and denial towards self. The following suggestions might help you continue on in a joyful attitude.

If you ever have a day where you are not cheerful, think on these things:

~Think of how God is changing your heart towards Him. Look at all the wonderful ways He is working in your life.

~Look back at the goals you have accomplished. Sit and write more goals for yourself and then talk to God about them in prayer.

~Concentrate on the family members you have around you right now. Do you have a mother and a father? You will not always have them with you, so think of how thankful you are for them. Do you have brothers and sisters around you? Thank God for them, as you will only live with them for a very short time.

~Stop thinking about yourself and think of one nice thing you can do for someone else today. Do you know a widow? Bake her something and go for a visit. Do you know an older person who is neglected? Take an hour and give it to them. Do you know children who are not raised with any Godly influence? Visit them and read them a Bible story.

~Do you have something that desperately needs to be finished? Put it at the top of your "to do" list! Start concentrating on what needs to be done, rather than on your own personal "feelings". That is going "inward"... Go "outward"!

~Determine only to do the Lord's will in your life at this moment. Do not let yourself fulfill "self".

Dearest sister, finding happiness in life is easy. It's simply how we live our life. We either, "find ourselves", as the world advises, and be miserable, or find true happiness and joy in giving our life away to others through serving them in Christ!

"For whosoever will save his life shall lose it; and whosoever will lose his life for my sake shall find it. For what is a man profited, if he shall gain the whole world, and lose his own soul? or what shall a man give in exchange for his soul." Matthew 16:25-26

Discussion:

~Name five things that make you happy.
~Are any of these things based upon dependence of the world?
~Are any of these things based upon giving yourself away?
~What is the difference between *pleasure* and *joy*?
~How does denying your flesh bring you joy?
~How does overcoming temptation bring you joy?
~Discuss the differences between the ways that nonbelievers obtain pleasure, and the ways a believer in Christ obtains true joy.
~How can you be truly happy?
~What should you do when you find yourself in an unhappy mood?
~Do you remember the Scripture that tells us what we are to think on?
~How can you encourage other young ladies to be truly happy?
~What should you do when you find someone who is telling you how unhappy they are? How could you help them?

RECOMMENDED RESOURCES:

HOMEMAKING:

Crowned With Silver, Biblical Femininity (Magazine) ~ Free Online. www.crownedwithsilver.com

Eat Healthy for $50 a Week - By Rhonda Barfield; Kensington Publishing Corp * 850 Third Avenue * New York, NY 10022

Miserly Moms, Living on One Income in a Two Income Economy - By Jonni McCoy; Full Quart Press * PO Box 254 * Elkton, MD * 21922-0254

HOMESCHOOLING:

LOGIC, The Right Use of Reason in the Inquiry after Truth - Written Isaac Watts; Soli Deo Gloria Publications * PO Box 451 * Morgan, PA * 15064

A Good Start - By Charles Haddon Spurgeon; Soli Deo Gloria Publications * PO Box 451 * Morgan, PA * 15064

Government Nannies - By Cathy Duffy (Gresham, Oregon: Noble Publishing Associates) Request from your local Christian book store.

How to Home School - By Gayle Graham (Melrose, Florida: Common Sense Press) Request from your local Christian book store.

Anyone Can Homeschool - By Terry Dorian, & Zan Peters Tyler; Hunting House Publishers * PO Box 53788 * Lafayette, LA 70505

How to Read a Book - By Mortimer Adler & Chalres Van Doren; A

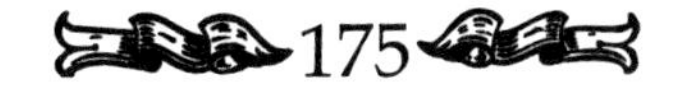

Touchtone Book; Simon & Schuster *Rockefeller Center * 1230 Avenue of Americs * New York, NY * 10020

WOMANHOOD:

The Pattern of Courtship - By Natali Miller; Canon Press; Moscow, Idaho

Waiting for Her Isaac - By Mr. & Mrs. Stephen B. Castleberry; Castleberry Farms Press * PO Box 337 * Poplar, WI 54864

Loving God with all Your Mind - By Elizabeth George; Harvest House Publishers * Eugene, OR 97402

Let Me Be a Woman - By Elisabeth Elliot; Back to the Bible Broadcasts * PO Box 82808 * Lincoln, NE 68501

A Woman After God's Own Heart - By Elizabeth George ; Harvest House Publishers * Eugene, OR 97402

The Little Girl's Treasure - compiled by Annie Brooks; Triangle Press * 23 5th Avenue SE * Conrad, MT * 59425

His Perfect Faithfulness, A Love Story Built by God - By Eric & Leslie Ludy; MAKARIOS Publishing Inc. * 3119 Concord Way * Longmont, CO 80503

Old-Fashioned Courtship & How it Works Today - by Jeff & Marge Barth; Parable Publishing House * RD 2, Box 2002 * Middlebury, VT 05753

ORGANIZATION:

Choreganizer; Steward Ship * PO Box 164 * Garden Valley, CA 95633

The Busy Woman's Daily Planner; 919 S. Main Street * Snowflake, AZ * 85937

Emilie's Household Hints - By Emilie Barnes; Harvest House Publishers * Eugene, OR 97402

MONEY MANAGEMENT:

Taming the Money Monster - By Ron Blue; Out of print, you can request it from an inter-library loan from your local library.

PARENTING:

Training Children in Godliness; Written by Jacob Abbott; Christian Liberty Press * 502 West Euclid Ave * Arlington Heights, IL * 60004

What is a Family - Written by Edith Schaeffer; Baker Book House Co. * Grand Rapids, MI 49516

The Christian Warrior - By Isaac Ambrose; Soli Deo Gloria Publications * PO Box 451 * Morgan, PA * 15064

PATTERNS:

FOLKWEAR PATTERNS, Old-fashioned and modest patterns. 2000 Riverside Drive #3 * Ashville, NC * 28804 E-mail info@folkwear.com

READING:

Just David & The Whole Hearted Child: Whole Heart Ministries * PO Box 67 * Walnut Springs, TX 76690 * 800-311-2146

****

Please understand that no book written by any human being today is 100% error free. The only book that we truly endorse is the Bible. Knowing this, we recommend these books for encouragements and help for women today even though they might not line up with exactly what we believe.

You, too, will probably not agree with every thought expressed in reading materials, but hopefully, the Lord has given you common sense and the power to reason according to the Scriptures, and you can be encouraged in some areas and toss out that which you do not believe. In other words, eat the meat and spit out the bones!

Remember to always read everything with a heart that will line everything up with God's Holy Word. Books are written by people, and those that love God are being perfected and taught by Him. Know that every person, even he who is putting out Christian reading material, is a *diamond in the rough*!

Again, hopefully you will be encouraged in Christian femininity by the preceding material list!

Yours in Christ,

A. B. Leaver & Friends
www.pearables.com

Notes

Notes

Notes

Our HOPE CHEST SERIES:
___Vol 1. Personal Help for Girls ~ $22.85 (Ages 9 - Up) (The Inside)
(Contains Bible study/Discussion at the end of each chapter)
___Vol 2. Preparing Your Hope Chest ~ $22.85 (Ages 9 - Up) (The Outside or The Doing)

___Personal Help for Boys Text ~ $22.85 (Ages 9- 109)
___Personal Help for Boys Companion Workbook~ $11.95
___Set of Personal Help for Boys Text and Workbook for $28

___Home Economics Level 1 - $18.95
___Home Economics Level 2 - $18.95
___Home Economics Level 3 - $18.95
___Set of 3 (one of each level) - $48

___Lessons in Responsibility Level 1 - $18.95 (Ages 6+)
___Lessons in Responsibility Level 2 - $18.95 (Ages 8+)
___Both books - Lessons in Responsibility Set - $35

_____Subtotal
____Shipping (Please add $3 for orders under $30. Please add 10% for orders over $30. Shipping out of U.S. please add 20% of order total.)
_____Total Enclosed

Name____
Address____
City_______________________State_______________Zip________

Please enclose payment to:

PEARABLES
P.O. Box 1071
Mukilteo, WA 98275

For sample pages go to:
www.pearables.com